Writing on the Job

A NORTON POCKET GUIDE

John C. Brereton
Margaret A. Mansfield

UNIVERSITY OF MASSACHUSETTS, BOSTON

W. W. NORTON & COMPANY

New York • London

Copyright © 1997 by W. W. Norton & Company, Inc.

All rights reserved
Printed in the United States of America
First Edition

The text of this book is composed in ITC Stone Serif and
Helvetica with the display set in Rockwell.
Composition by University Graphics, Inc.

The chart on p. 3 is adapted from *Open to Language: A New
College Rhetoric* by Patrick Hartwell and Robert H. Bentley.
Copyright © 1982 by Oxford University Press. Reprinted by
permission.

Library of Congress Cataloging-in-Publication Data
Brereton, John C.
    Writing on the job : a Norton pocket guide / Brereton
John C., Margaret A. Mansfield.
        p. cm.
    Includes index.
    1. Business writing.   2. Technical writing.   3. Resumes
(Employment)   4. Editing.   5. English language—Business
English.
I. Mansfield, Margaret A.   II. Title.
HF5718.3.B74   1997
808'.0666—dc20   96-10542

ISBN 0-393-97089-2 spiral-bound
      0-393-03969-2 cloth

W. W. Norton & Company, Inc., 500 Fifth Avenue, New
    York, N.Y. 10110   http://web.wwnorton.com
W. W. Norton & Company Ltd., 10 Coptic Street, London
    WC1A 1PU

2 3 4 5 6 7 8 9 0

CONTENTS

Contents

Contents

About This Book

We've arranged this book to help anyone faced with a practical writing task. In it you'll find specific advice on everything from resumes to minutes to news stories to publicity releases. It's organized simply. The first part has nine chapters containing the most commonly used formats; each chapter demonstrates the requirements of the format, shows how to shape your writing, and supplies some possible variations. The remaining chapters make up a brief writer's guide explaining issues that go beyond individual formats and providing information about where to look for additional help.

Unlike many books, then, this one provides most of its information and advice in the samples and examples; the rest of the text serves to support those examples.

We've structured this book around formats and examples, because that's how most on-the-job writers learn their craft. If you're asked to write a fundraising letter, chances are someone will point you toward files full of similar letters sent by your organization in the past. You'll read a number of them, begin to discern a pattern, and develop your own mental or written guidelines for the form. Along the way, you'll also find examples of approaches you like or dislike, and you'll get ideas for new strategies and variations on the form. To recreate this workplace experience, we've filled our chapters with examples you should examine thoughtfully to see how they both follow and vary the conventions of a format.

Although formats are central to our approach, you'll find you can't learn a format without becoming engaged in strategy and process. A format is more than a container for your content; it's a way of making ideas accessible to a reader by presenting them in a familiar order and layout. And in another sense, a format is a way to investigate a topic, a kind of checklist that helps you generate the information your readers expect.

Like much workplace writing, this book represents the collaborative efforts of more than just its co-authors. Our interns and the students in our advanced professional writing courses at the University of Massachusetts, Boston, have given us insight into writing on the job in a wide range of settings from the state capitol to advertising and public relations firms to newspapers to nonprofit theater companies. Those interns gave us the initial rationale for this book: we wanted a book we could hand them, something that would show them the formats they'd be working with day by day.

Scholars and teachers of professional writing have helped us with specific advice: Davida Charney (Pennsylvania State University), Margaret Graham (Iowa State University), Polly Marshall (Hinds Community College), Michael Munley (Ball State University), Nell Ann Pickett (Hinds Community College), James E. Porter (Purdue University), and Scott P. Sanders (University of New Mexico) offered thoughtful comments drawn from their considerable expertise and experience. We've had help from professional writers in the Boston area: Rebecca Saunders of Write, Inc., Mary Frakes of Fidelity Investments, and Michelle McPhee of the *Boston Globe* all examined our book with an eye toward their own workplaces. At W. W. Norton & Company, we've had valuable help from Jane Carter, Diane O'Connor, Kate Lovelady, Marian Johnson, and Gigi Madore, and from our editor, Carol Hollar-Zwick, who gave us the encouragement and criticism we needed. And at home our spouses have given both emotional and professional support. George Mansfield has been a source for writing about urban planning and local government and politics, and Virginia Brereton, herself a writer, has provided help with matters of tone and phrasing.

Introduction

Whenever anyone thinks about how writing actually gets done, Hollywood has plenty of false lessons to teach. Who hasn't stared in wonder as television's or the movies' idea of a reporter—Lois Lane comes to mind—sits at a keyboard and bangs out a perfectly crafted story at breakneck speed? That, we are expected to believe, is real-world writing, the way pros like reporters do it.

We contrast this image with Hollywood's picture of the starving writer in a garret, painfully facing that blank sheet of paper while waiting for the muse to descend or endlessly crumpling up false starts and tossing them on the floor. Real literature, the movies tell us, is tough work. As Hollywood would have it, reporters, the real pros, turn out terrific stories on the spot, while poets or novelists, true artists, wrestle with their words till inspiration strikes.

Both views, experience tells us, are equally unrealistic depictions of how most writers actually go about their trade. In fact, Hollywood's idea of what writers and artists really do is most likely based on previous movies, on folklore, or on rumor. The true picture is both more and less interesting. Some days both author and reporter cruise right along, writing quickly, line after line. Other days both are simply stuck—can't write a word. In fact, all people dealing with words, whether as art or craft, share more similarities than differences. And artists and craftspeople have plenty in common with the people we think of as the most likely readers of our book: everyone who needs to write for an organization or who has to confront the requirements of writing for publication.

The Writing Process

Within the last two decades, researchers at universities have begun to understand what separates successful writers from un-

1

successful ones. One of the biggest differences is that successful writers are much more effective at using the different components of the writing process. What are these components? They are simply steps or stages that almost all successful writers go through. Most researchers describe five stages:

1. planning and information gathering
2. drafting
3. revising
4. editing
5. proofreading

One insight from university research is that successful writers do not simply follow these stages in a linear manner: reading over a draft or getting feedback on it from a co-worker may call for additional planning; revising may reveal the need for more information; difficulty in editing for word choice may lead to the realization that a whole section needs to be reconceived. In short, it's wisest to think of writing as a process that constantly loops back on itself:

The loops reflect the way you and most good writers usually operate. While planning, you might hit on a neat way to phrase an idea and jot it down. Similarly, when you finish a rough draft, you might read it over and decide you need some additional planning. Or when revising you might notice that one important part of an argument is missing, so you go back and draft some more.

The flowchart on the next page looks daunting, as if writing were some enormously complex production. But the single most powerful insight of two decades of research into writing is that writers shouldn't try to do everything at once but instead should focus on a single stage, or a couple of related stages, at a time. It's especially important to defer almost all the editing and proofreading till the end, when you're sure of the shape and focus of the document you need to polish. Yes, you can correct a typo as you pause to collect your thoughts, but don't let a concern for mechanical correctness or for finding the exact word constantly interrupt your flow as you shape a draft.

Many expert writers defer another daunting task, writing the introduction, as well. Why? They've learned to wait until they see what they've said, since it's hard to introduce an idea you haven't yet worked out in detail. So if you get stuck about how to begin, don't begin at the beginning. Jump into the middle—the specifics—and wait till after you've found those specifics taking shape to draft your introduction.

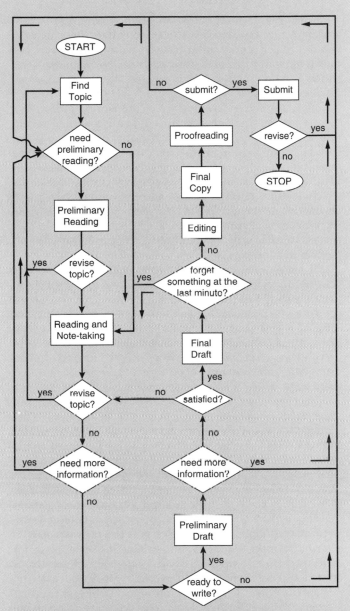

Adapted from Pat Hartwell, *Open to Language* (New York: Oxford, 1987).

Inexperienced writers think extensive revising is a sign of weakness, that experienced or talented writers get it right the first time. Such a view, most likely based on the movies, has caused millions to avoid drafting and revision. But most expert writers write multiple drafts of nearly everything they do, sometimes as many as six or seven.

Experts also focus on one stage of the writing process at a time. When they write a draft, they do only that; they refrain from checking their work or editing or proofreading. When they revise an early draft they look for large-scale issues like organization and coverage of important topics. Later, when they have a satisfactory draft, they edit by focusing on sentence structure and tone. And almost all professionals save proofreading for the final stage. (Newspapers and publishers value this separation of proofreading and editing so highly that they employ separate staffs of editors and proofreaders in order to produce first-rate copy.)

This professional separation of roles offers a key to making your writing successful: the understanding that, though all writing usually goes through a version of those five stages, most people are better at some than at others. Plenty of people can come up with a potential idea, but can't shape it terribly well. Many others are excellent at revising someone else's work. And we've all known people who have a perfect command of grammar or who can spot tiny errors. Very few people are terrific at every stage, which is why professional publishers have such a clear division of labor and why much workplace writing is to some extent collaborative.

An author, say a biographer, first discusses a subject and an approach with a publisher, who offers a contract based on the writer's idea, a sample chapter or two, and a rough sense of what the finished product will look like. When the author finishes a couple of drafts and submits a revised version, it's sent to an editor, who helps shape its larger sections or who perhaps suggests a different order for the chapters. After the author completes another draft, the manuscript goes to a copy editor, who edits the language, word by word and sentence by sentence, for correctness and appropriate style. And finally, the book is printed in proofs, which get inspected by proofreaders for typographical errors. So in some professional settings, writers get a support system that frees them to concentrate on one stage at a time. It's that system of isolating the stages that makes so much published writing well shaped, smooth, and accurate.

But many professionals who write don't get such a full support system, so you and most workplace writers will be responsible for all five stages, especially in everyday writing with a tight deadline. By focusing on one stage at a time, allowing even a five-minute coffee break before editing and proofreading, and knowing when you absolutely need to ask for help, you can put professional principles to work in your own writing.

So does the Hollywood image of the reporter have even a smidgen of truth? Yes, some very experienced writers working in a thoroughly familiar genre—like real-life top reporters—can produce stories in one short burst of energy. But what looks like instant creativity is in fact only the outward, visible sign of an internalized writing process that includes all the stages we've identified above. Moreover, much of their facility comes from having in mind a format, or template, of what the finished product will look like. Reporters, for instance, know that any news story will have a lead of 35 or so words that gets readers interested and an order that follows one of a limited number of organizational plans. As they shape a story in their heads, they are already marshalling the facts into one of these familiar patterns. You can take a cue from reporters by using some of the templates and conventions in the chapters that follow and by learning others in the context of your particular business or group.

So the principles to take away from the professional writing process are: first, develop your own strategies for composing by learning to keep stages distinct and working on one thing at a time, and, second, master the conventions and formats of the writing you will do frequently.

Planning a Draft

As many writers will tell you, the hardest part is often planning a draft that shows promise for development. Publicity writers seek inspiration, reporters look desperately for a lead, columnists search for ideas. In more everyday settings like those covered in this book, it may seem that the occasion, audience, and purpose for writing are given and that the task at hand is simply to develop prose appropriate for all three.

But the "givens" can be tricky, and a wise writer learns not to take anything for granted, to ask a lot of questions before starting. Do you fully understand the **occasion** for the proposal you've been asked to write? What has happened recently to make this proposal timely? What are the politics of the situation? Is the **purpose** clear when your supervisor asks you to write a press release for local papers about how your company will be featured in a national business journal article? Did she have in mind general good PR for the company? publicity for the specific program or innovation featured in the journal article? payback to the journal by giving it some local press? Finally, who are your **readers**? Are the instructions you'll write aimed at experts, novices, or a mix? Is a new dress-code policy statement likely to encounter enthusiasm or resentment from readers? If you aren't confident of the answers to these questions, you're likely to feel like Hollywood's starving writer, bogged down in false starts because different occasions, purposes, and audiences demand different approaches, different orders of ideas.

This may sound a bit overwhelming, but a colleague of ours who consults for large corporations has developed a simple yet strikingly effective means of getting started on a letter, memo, or report: she calls it "the important telephone call." Imagine that you need to make a crucial call to a valued supporter or colleague. If you're like most efficient people, you decide in advance what items you need to cover. You take out a sheet of paper and list them. Which should come first? second? last? How should you introduce each item?

As you decide on the answers to these questions, you're quite consciously connecting the occasion and your purpose with your audience. Are you trying to raise money from a longtime supporter? You'll probably begin by acknowledging past generosity, plead the present need, and ask for a specific amount. Are you asking a favor from reluctant colleagues? You might start with a reminder of how you've helped them in the past or begin by offering to do something about one of their recurrent complaints before you pose your question. Are you responding to a colleague's urgent request for key facts? You'll skip the preamble and get right to the point. Analyzing these occasions and audiences has not only affected the order of items on your original list but also caused you to add things, like the acknowledgment of the contributor's past generosity and the tit-for-tat offer to address a colleague's complaint. You may not actually rewrite your list before calling, but knowing the situation and audience allows you to tailor your approach to each call.

This little bit of preparation for a phone call, something most of us have done, is exactly the kind of planning you need to do for a successful first draft. And in this age when most people tend to think first of face-to-face or telephone encounters, imagining a letter or memo as a phone call may be just the thing to get you started. You've made plenty of calls and planned some of them in advance. After making sure you have answered the questions about occasion, purpose, and audience (perhaps after consultation with colleagues or your boss), just write down, whether in paragraph or list form, everything you need to cover. That's your plan, and when you flesh it out in rough sentences and paragraphs, you'll have a first draft. Of course, you'll still need to revise one or more times. And even after you're happy with what you've said, you'll need to get down to the nitty-gritty of editing and proofreading so that every detail of spelling and punctuation will be correct in the final copy. (See our Writer's Guide for more help on these stages.) But making the plan is usually what gets you over the hump and on the way.

So far, then, we have two bits of advice: make the writing process work for you, and use the model of the important phone call to develop a writing plan. These are especially good ways of getting started. The third piece of advice, which operates at every stage of the writing task, depends on the simple yet powerful distinction between saying and doing. Any letter you write can *tell* the reader that you're sorry—that's saying. A good letter will make the reader *believe* that you're sorry—that's doing. So any memo or letter you write will be saying something. But more importantly, your writing will inevitably do something as well, leave an impression or cause the reader to act in a certain way. A careless letter will leave the impression that you don't know much about writing or don't care much about the reader. A poorly organized memo may say all the important things, but it won't do what matters most: persuade the reader to approve, understand, or cooperate.

The first chapter presents a letter that confronts exactly this dilemma, how to convey the writer's intentions about the situation at hand on paper (see Sample 4, p. 18). More importantly, everything in this book is about how your writing will affect and influence the reader. The emphasis is on you, the writer, coming into contact with the formats, or templates, necessary to get things done. Throughout, we'll emphasize the choices you'll face and your opportunities to make the different formats work for you, to do what's appropriate to your occasion, purpose, and audience.

Formats and Contexts

Our book supplies the most commonly used formats for on-the-job writing. But the challenge comes in fitting the format into the right context or adjusting the format to the needs of the setting in which it will be used. An example here will show what we mean.

One of our chapters contains a format for an agenda, along with suggestions for how to list the topics of an upcoming meeting. The agenda on page 138 is a good model: it's the one used by many organizations large and small; it has stood the test of time. Still, that precise format may not be exactly what you need. Why not? Because before you were assigned the agenda, Arlene M., the long-term company secretary/treasurer, had been doing agendas in her own idiosyncratic way for fifteen years. She developed a method that people in your company have become used to. You, the new agenda maker, cannot simply barge in and replace a time-tested format. It doesn't matter whether your agenda is better or more authoritative. "Better" is what works in your setting, and besides, Arlene has just become vice president. Are you really going to junk her model and impose a format you found in a book? Over time you can make changes, but not without giving the issue some thought.

Anyone in an office setting has to think about the appropriateness of format to context; we think context should always come first. Throughout this book we've tried to be sensitive to the situation of a real workplace, with the inevitable personal investments in formats. Thus, we have provided both the format that usually works best and the principles behind it, so you'll know what parts of the format should be adopted as is and what parts can be changed to suit your own setting.

Plenty of books or computer programs can hand you a template and tell you to fill in the blanks. For instance, Microsoft Word has some nifty agenda models. So do other programs and books you can buy. But what *Writing on the Job* supplies is both models and rationales. Yes, by all means continue with Arlene's old quirky model pretty much as is, but make a change here and a change there and over time her model will have been adjusted to fit your agenda perfectly. (Try another scenario: Arlene has finally retired, and you're in charge of minutes because people want "new ideas." Then by all means junk her old agenda model and propose a brand new one. You'll get praised for your boldness. What was a bad move in one context is a good one in another.)

Understanding the context helps you decide how much of the format to include. This applies to press releases, brochures, resumes, and newsletters. Are you applying for a job as a math teacher? You don't want your resume to look like one more appropriate for an art director at an upscale department store. (One reason is that the readers of your resume are likely to be math teachers!) Are you doing the monthly newsletter for your local environmental action group? With an inexpensive desktop publishing program you can turn out a professional-looking newsletter, filled with dazzling graphics, the classiest fonts, and the latest in special effects. But ask yourself, do the group members want something so fancy? The dazzling look of a professional publishing program sends its own message, and it may not be compatible with the group's grassroots activism.

So context is all. Communicative needs depend on that old triangle of writer, audience, and message. A good writer never gets too far ahead of the audience. And this book will help you adjust modern publishing capabilities to the real world of readers, so they will pay attention to what you have to say.

1
Letters and Memos

Letters and memos represent the most common forms of writing and perhaps the most traditional. Who hasn't had to write a letter? And what person in a business or organizational setting hasn't had to write a memo?

The requirements for some letters and memos are fairly flexible, indicating that writers have been able to stretch and adapt the basic formats to suit their needs. Yet some requirements still apply. This chapter provides a guide to the most commonly used forms: letters in traditional and block formats; customer service, bad news, and fundraising letters; and formal and informal memos. Writers familiar with these formats and some strategies for adapting them can handle just about any kind of letter or memo the situation demands.

1a Letters

In matters of format, traditional business letters allow the least room for creativity; you must follow the conventions that your readers expect. There are two basic types: traditional format, with indented address and closing, and block format, with everything aligned at the left margin.

Modern practice follows the block format more and more, while the traditional format is most common for friendly letters or letters that are not written on business stationery.

OHIO INDUSTRIAL PRODUCTS
440 COATS ROAD
CLEVELAND, OH 33344

May 12, 1996

Mr. Arnold Sternglass, President
Mid-West Corporate Design
400 Lincoln Road
Columbus, IN 43332-1223

Dear Mr. Sternglass:

We are a mid-sized polymer and coatings manufacturer founded in
1979. We are revamping our corporate communication and publicity
materials and would like Mid-West to bid on our new stationery.

In particular, we would like samples of your different types of paper
and envelopes. The numbers and titles are from your spring 1996
catalog:

Defender	# 12206
Patrician	# 13005
Kent	# 14220

We would also be interested in engaging a Mid-West consultant to
help us design a new company logo and plan the look of our publicity
materials. I have enclosed samples of our current letterhead and envelopes.

Would you please send us a fee schedule for such a consultation
and ask one of your representatives to call on us this month?

Thank you very much for your help.

Yours truly,

Priscilla Barnes

Priscilla Barnes
Assistant Vice President

jk/PB
Enclosures
cc: Bernice Hausfelt
    Alfred Hoffman

Letter Format

Business letters should be single spaced on $8\frac{1}{2} \times 11$ inch letterhead, with $1\frac{1}{2}$ inch margins all around. (With very short letters, the top margin can be increased to center the text on the page.)

Sample 1 is in block format, so everything begins at the left margin. (See Sample 5, p. 19, for a letter in traditional format, where address and closing are indented.)

DATE   Month (spelled out), day (followed by a comma), year

INSIDE ADDRESS   The inside address belongs two lines after the date; this is the same address that appears on the envelope and includes:

- the recipient's name preceded by "Mr.," "Ms.," "Professor," "Dr.," etc.
- title of office ("President"), following the name on the same line, if the title is short. (A longer title, such as "Vice President for Public Affairs," would go on the next line.)
- full address—street, city, state (official abbreviation only), ZIP code.

SALUTATION   "Dear Mr. Sternglass:"—title, last name, colon.
NOTE: *If you don't know whether the person to whom you are addressing the letter is a man or a woman, use the full name and omit the title—"Dear Leslie Martin"—or use a generic description—"Dear Goodyear," "Dear Town Manager." Save "To Whom It May Concern" for recommendations and testimonials, and avoid "Gentlemen" and "Dear Sir"; they're sexist.*

BODY   The body of the letter uses short, single-spaced paragraphs. State the purpose for writing and any connection with the recipient in the first paragraph—"We . . . would like Mid-West to bid." Describe what's wanted in the middle of the letter's body, and request specific action at the end of the body: "Please send . . . and ask one of your representatives to call."

CLOSE   Insert the close two lines below the last line of the letter. Capitalize the first word; conclude with a comma: "Yours truly,"

SIGNATURE   Leave three lines of space after the close for the signature; the name should be signed in ink with the signatory's name typed one line below and the title typed one line below that.

TYPIST'S INITIALS If the letter is typed by someone other than the writer, then the typist's initials should be inserted below the typed name of the signatory; capitalize the writer's initials, and use lower case for the typist's—jk/PB (or PB:jk).

ENCLOSURES "Enclosures" (or "Encl.") indicates that additional material should be included; you could also list enclosures—"Enclosed: current letterhead and envelopes."

COPIES List other recipients alphabetically (or by rank)—
cc: Bernice Hausfelt
    Alfred Hoffman

Writing Business Letters

While no two kinds of business letters are exactly alike, there are certain features besides format that they share. Because business folk value their time, business letters must get to the point quickly; they should be brief but clear. The relationship between the writer and the recipient should be set forth at the outset. If action on the part of the recipient is requested, then that action should be specified—don't beat about the bush. If background is needed, then it should be given briefly in the body of the letter, mentioning only those points that are relevant to the reader. If your letter is a response, then it should mention the date of the letter, phone call, or meeting that prompted your response.

The tone of business letters is also fairly uniform; letters to people with whom you've worked closely for several years may be appropriately friendly, but business correspondence in general tends toward the formal. And no matter how caustic the person you're responding to, your tone should be polite, your response measured. Why? because an underlying motivation in writing business letters is usually to establish or reestablish a positive working relationship: with letters of complaint, to smooth the waters; with bad news letters, to encourage the recipients to accept the bad news with as little ill will as possible.

Sent from home rather than a business office, this letter uses a variation of the traditional format used for friendly letters, with address, date, and close on the right, but with no indentations at the openings of paragraphs.

Adds extra space at top to center vertically on page

211 Amboy Road
Hutchison, KS 12222
May 11, 1996

Ms. Amy Bascom, Parent Coordinator
Bascom Consolidated School Board
48 Main Street
Lawrence, KS 12223

Follows name with title, preceded by comma

Dear Ms. Bascom:

Follows salutation with colon

I am planning to move to Lawrence at the end of August and will be enrolling my two children, ages 9 and 11, in local schools. I need to know the following:

1. What documents should my husband and I send to you from the old school?
2. Does the Lawrence school district offer bus service? How far away does one have to live to be eligible?
3. What special programs or magnet schools are available, and what are the deadlines for applying?
4. What are the dates for new student enrollment?

Lists specific requests to make them easy to follow

Thank you for your help.

Sincerely yours,

Arlene Rambeau

Arlene Rambeau

Capitalizes first word of closing; follows closing with comma

15

This letter, written by one merchant on behalf of a group, aims at convincing a police official that enforcement of a parking ordinance has been lax and needs to be stepped up. In block style, everything is flush left except for the letterhead.

MEDICAL SUPPLY CENTER
III MAIN STREET
OLDTOWN, MA 01614

September 20, 1995

Ms. Athene Poulakis
Oldtown Traffic Department
18 Sycamore Street
Oldtown, MA 01211

Dear Ms. Poulakis:

States complaint and request for help concisely; identifies writer as representing group

On behalf of the merchants in the 100-block of Main Street, I would like to express serious concern about the lack of enforcement of the 30-minute parking limit. We are losing business because our patrons can't find convenient parking, and we need your help.

Gives brief history to show past efforts to solve problem

At our request, the 30-minute zone was created in April 1993 to prevent long-term employee and commuter parking on this block, so that patrons would have easy access to our shops for short errands.

Supports complaint with specific evidence

In the first year after the zone was established, parking officers patrolled the area and ticketed violators several times each day. Since then, however, enforcement has become quite sporadic, and violations have dramatically increased. In the last two weeks, Adele Douglas of Sports, Inc., Herb Wiley of Wiley Foods, and I have monitored the block closely. Since September 5, we have seen a parking officer issuing tickets only once, and we have recorded 17 instances of cars parked on the block for two to five hours.

Calls for specific action

I know I speak for Adele, Herb, and all the merchants on this block in urging you to take immediate steps to address this threat to our economic health by strictly enforcing the 30-minute parking limit on our block.

Sincerely,

Martin Wetherall

Martin Wetherall, Manager

The writer of Sample 4, Superintendent Shannon Weaver, could have had many overt motivations in answering the complaint she received. She might have wanted to get an irate complainer off her back, to fulfill her job requirements, which include answering citizen complaints, to express her genuine unhappiness because a job took longer than planned, or to be nice to Ms. Robinson, who knows everyone important in town, including Weaver's boss.

While it is possible that Shannon Weaver had all four of these motives for writing, she wouldn't want to convey only the first two. She wouldn't want to make Ms. Robinson feel that this matter was routine and that Weaver handled it in a callous, unfeeling way, answering it only because she had to. That is *not* the way to smooth the waters. What any intelligent public or private official wants is to make the recipient believe that the complaint has been listened to and taken seriously. That is precisely what Sample 4 attempts to do, and it communicates this concern by tracking down the cause of the problem. This is a case where an apology would not be enough; neither would an attempt to fix things, since the complaint is about late repairs, not incomplete or shoddy workmanship. In this case the explanation makes all the difference. Will the letter work to mollify the irate citizen? There is no guarantee. But at least it attempts to do the right thing, to make the citizen understand that the office holder has taken the complaint seriously.

What makes readers believe they are being listened to? First and simplest, they need to see that the writer understands the problem. In the case of Sample 4, the writer followed a time-tested strategy: open the letter with a straightforward restatement of the problem, a brief summary of the letter of complaint. If this summary is accurate, the writer feels she has been understood. (Correspondingly, if it's inaccurate, then the writer thinks the reader doesn't care or doesn't understand the situation.) This restatement meets a simple human need to know that the complaint has been registered. If so, the official is well on the way to satisfying the citizen.

Sample 5 lets residents know about an unwelcome fee increase. What should such a letter do? The writers of the letter, a condominium board, chose to do two things:

1. make the residents understand the reason for the rise;
2. make the residents see that, even with the rise, they were paying less than their neighbors.

While the letter explains that there is no way to avoid the in-

This customer service letter is a reply to "hate mail," the kind of complaint that must be answered calmly and politely. The writer, a town official, has received a complaint from an influential citizen whose driveway was blocked by road construction two weeks longer than planned. The letter is in block format, with everything flush left.

TOWN OF RHINEBECK CLIFFS
DEPARTMENT OF TRANSPORTATION
VALHALLA, NY 11333

Uses block format: all lines begin at left margin; double space left between new paragraphs (paragraphs not indented)

September 21, 1995

Ms. Isabelle Robinson
221 Allagash Drive
Valhalla, NY 11333

Dear Ms. Robinson:

Acknowledges problem concisely

Thank you for your August 19 letter pointing out that the culvert work near your driveway was not finished until two weeks after the date promised, August 1.

Expresses regret

I understand your concern, and we deeply regret the inconvenience you suffered.

Explains problem's cause, showing that writer has undertaken investigation on complainant's behalf

I thought you deserved an explanation, so I asked the contractor, ASCO Construction, to account for the delay. Their job foreman told me that the delay was strictly the result of an unforeseen complication with a gas line. It was marked incorrectly on their maps and had to be moved. ASCO uncovered the gas line on July 22 but had to wait until August 9 for the gas company crew to come and relocate it. When the line finally was moved, construction of the culverts proceeded on schedule.

Restates regret simply

I know this doesn't make up for the inconvenience, but I wanted you to know exactly what contributed to the delay.

Aligns close at left

Yours truly,

Leaves three lines of space for signature

Shannon Weaver
Shannon Weaver
Superintendent

Sets job title one line below writer's name

Here the writer has to present unwelcome information in the best possible light. The format is traditional, with indented first lines of paragraphs, and date and close to the right.

CULLODEN TOWERS
A CONDOMINIUM COMMUNITY
3000 CAMINO REAL
BOCA RATON, FLORIDA 98212

March 24, 1996

Dear Fellow Resident:

Over the past three years Culloden Towers has enjoyed excellent service at a cost lower than the prevailing rates in this part of Boca Raton. Through careful planning, the condominium board has managed to achieve savings in spite of difficult economic conditions.

Sets stage with positive view of organization

We are happy to report that we can continue to provide first-class service, but unfortunately we are no longer able to avoid a fee increase. Accordingly, at the March meeting your directors unanimously authorized an across-the-board, 6 percent increase in condominium fees for the 1996–97 fiscal year.

States bad news simply, with no attempt to hide increase

Your directors know that any increase in fees is unwelcome. However, this 6 percent increase was necessitated by three specific new situations:

1. a new labor contract with maintenance staff that calls for an 8 percent wage increase,
2. an increase of over 5 percent in town taxes,
3. an increase of over 8 percent in utility costs.

Sets forth reasons for rise clearly, numbered and indented to make them easy to follow

You will note that 6 percent is below the average of previous increases. It is also below the increases on comparable condominiums in the area. Culloden Towers still costs less per month than comparable buildings.

Makes favorable comparison with other condominiums

Your directors have worked very hard to find savings that can offset the increases we inevitably face. We will continue to work hard in the future to provide first-class service at a price all residents can afford.

Pledges to serve residents well in future

Sincerely,

Lyman Abbot

Lyman Abbot
Secretary

Fund-raising letters are at the heart of direct-mail campaigns. This letter is from one prominent member of a city's business community to another; it is more personal than most business letters, since the writer and recipient know each other.

BARTLETT SAVINGS BANK
211 ABLESON DRIVE
BARTLETT, OK 67890

May 27, 1996

Mr. Abner Duckett, President
Duckett Oil Corporation
Duckett Building
Bartlett, OK 67890

Dear Mr. Duckett:

Links current request to previous generosity

I'm writing in my capacity as chair of the annual Bartlett Oklahoma Fund Drive, which will kick off at the end of June. I know we've been able to count on you and your company in the past for a generous contribution. Duckett Oil has been one of our strongest supporters.

Names specific amount and provides rationale for request

This year I'm asking whether you would be willing to join the select few who have become members of the Chairman's Club for a contribution of $5,000. That is double your generous pledge of last year, but it is just what we need to get the fund off to a strong start. If you and other civic leaders join the Chairman's Club, it will make the best possible impression on everyone concerned. And if we can tell donors that the town's leading citizens like yourself have pitched in with $5,000, then they will have an easier time giving a substantial amount as well.

As you know, the money will go to the best possible causes, all right here in Bartlett: the Symphony, the Masonic Hospital, the homeless shelter, and the Youth Opportunity Center.

Promises follow-up telephone call

Can I count on you to pledge at the Chairman's Club level? I'll call you next Thursday to get your response.

Sincerely,

Ernest Sugg

Ernest Sugg
Vice President

crease, at least it offers a reasonable explanation for it. Residents would believe that the board examined the situation carefully and arranged for the lowest possible increase, that the board's hope was to keep the residents content, if not exactly to make them happy.

The letter attempts to demonstrate that the board of directors understands the residents' needs, has the situation under control, and is still committed to providing good service.

1b Memos

Memos are the heart of an organization's internal communications. As a general rule, letters go to people outside the organization, memos to people within. (There are exceptions; some formal correspondence to an organization's members goes in letter form, but memos rarely go to people outside.)

The range of memos is just as wide as the range of letters. A memo can be anything from a quick couple of words dashed on a scrap of paper to a very formal, multiple page memorandum on official stationery. But no matter how formal or informal, memos deserve a writer's full attention. After all, the writer is on display in a memo just as much as in a letter.

The memo format is the one to use for most short reports and proposals as well. Though many organizations have specific printed forms (like travel expense and incident reports), in many cases a simple memo can do the job, as some of the sample memos in this chapter illustrate.

Despite the structural differences between memos and letters and the differences in the audience for the two formats, what works for a successful letter will work in a memo as well: write multiple drafts without premature editing, organize the first draft as if you were planning an important phone call, and think first of what the writing needs to do, not what it needs to say.

This is the latest in a series of memos on the subject. For something as important as a smoking ban, employees need to be prepared far in advance.

ENDERBEE ENTERPRISES
TOOLS FOR THE BUSY WORKPLACE

MEMORANDUM

TO: All Employees **DATE:** October 5, 1996
FROM: A. E. Ness, **SUBJECT:** Smoking
Manager Regulations

As you know, beginning today smoking will be prohibited inside all Enderbee buildings.

Enderbee has ended indoor smoking in order to ensure a safe workplace. The decision grew out of a series of employer-union meetings that began last February and is an example of employee-management cooperation.

Smokers will find areas set aside outside each main office building. Follow the signs labelled "Employee Smoking," and look for the blue paint on the asphalt. Please use the ashtrays. All smoking areas are sheltered from snow and rain but are still exposed to the cold weather.

For the many employees who wish to quit smoking, cessation clinics will begin on October 15. The times and places of the sessions are listed on the attached brochure; times and places have also been posted on all bulletin boards. Additionally, Enderbee health-care coverage will pay up to $175 to any employee who successfully completes the smoking cessation program at St. Joseph's Hospital or at the Rossville hypnotherapy center.

The new no-smoking policy will make the workplace safer for everyone, and we hope that all Enderbee employees will cooperate fully.

Memo Format

Sample 7 is a formal memorandum, printed on the company's standard memo form and sent to all the employees of a large company on a subject that has been under discussion for quite a while. Some organizations allow leeway in the format of memos, while others require a rigid pattern. This memo shares certain definite parts with other formal memorandums.

HEADING The heading includes:

- the sender's full name and title. (Informal memos use first names only—see Sample 8, p. 24.)
- recipients' full names and titles, but "All Employees" is the sensible alternative here.
- date—month (spelled out), day (followed by a comma), year.
- subject (sometimes "Re:")—information on this line should be brief but specific. "Regulations" or even "New regulations" would be too general.

BODY The body of the memo should be made up of short, focused paragraphs. Sample 7 states the point of the memo at the outset, gives a brief justification and run-down of the history behind the memo in paragraph 2, tells readers exactly how to find new smoking areas and offers two kinds of help with quitting in paragraphs 3 and 4, and concludes on a positive note, encouraging cooperation.

Writing Memos

Memos tend to have very clearly defined parts. Some of the parts, like the heading, are so rigidly determined that most organizations have printed memo forms, usually both large and small. Such forms generally have headings with spaces for the sender's name, the recipient's name, the date, and the subject. In formal memos, senders use their full names and titles, listing recipients by their full names and titles as well; in informal memos just first names are expected for both.

The date should include the month (spelled out), the day (followed by a comma), and the year. Most memo forms have a space for the date, but many writers not locked into this format prefer to place the date before the heading (above the sender and recipient information) to prevent readers from confusing the date of the memo with other dates in the body.

The subject (sometimes listed in the heading as "Re") should be stated concisely but explicitly. "Contracts," for example, would be too vague for a memo about new contracts that have just come in on four books a publishing company is about to begin working on. Something like "Four new book contracts" would be better. The reader shouldn't have to get to the body of the memo before knowing what it's about.

While the body of the memo is not usually decreed by a form, some general rules govern this part as well. The message in the body should, again, be short and focused. One-page memos are becoming increasingly popular with busy managers, who like everything to be concise. If more material is needed, it can go in supporting documents or in an accompanying report.

SAMPLE 8: ROUTINE, INFORMAL MEMO

This memo conveys all the necessary information about a routine matter, the time and place of the monthly budget meeting. (In many cases this same memo is circulated on E-mail as well. The format and style would be the same.) The group has met before; members call each other by first names. For Arnie to use his full name and title—Arnold M. Wasserstein, Deputy Regional Director of Planning, Consolidated School District of Twin Lakes—in an informal memo would be unnecessary and regarded by some as pompous. But a very formal memo or report would demand full name and title; otherwise he'd be seen as too casual.

MEMORANDUM

TO:	Budget Group Members (Ken, Marge, and Tom)
FROM:	Arnie W.
DATE:	November 19, 1995
RE:	End of month budget meeting on November 27

Lists recipients and sender by first name

We'll meet in the south conference room on Friday, November 27, from 10:00 to 11:00.

Presents purpose explicitly, along with special requirements for meeting

Purpose: to prepare forecasts for upcoming quarter.
Please bring your spreadsheets and calculators.

Special topic: new reporting requirements for December.

Those who like one-page memos often want the most important material to come first: result or recommendation or new policy at the outset, rationale or supporting reasons later. If the memo is in response to an earlier request, refer to that request and its date in the opening sentence. If the memo makes recommendations, put them at the beginning (see Sample 39, p. 110). Sample 7 (p. 22), for example, states the company's new no-smoking rule in the first sentence; Sample 8 (p. 24) states the memo's purpose—"to prepare forecasts for the upcoming quarter"—at the outset as well.

Like a business letter, a memo needs to be explicit about what it wants the reader to do: make a decision, expect a confirming phone call, authorize a payment, and so forth. Novice memo writers often fail to be clear about what readers are supposed to do. You shouldn't be bashful in a memo. Sample 7, for example, tells employees exactly how to find the new smoking areas and offers two kinds of help for those wishing to quit; Sample 8 asks recipients specifically to bring spreadsheets and calculators, and tells them exactly where and when they'll meet.

2
News and Feature Stories

Like any other kind of writing, journalism has its own rules, styles, and conventions. And the kind of writing we're calling journalistic extends well beyond what news you're familiar with from the newspaper. Journalistic style serves as a model for a whole range of writing: news stories for radio or television, press releases, feature articles for publicity, news or feature articles for internal or external newsletters, reports of meetings, and announcements of organizational or policy changes. In addition, the principles of good journalistic style apply to many other types of writing done for groups and organizations. If you can handle newspaper style, you can manage most other writing formats.

2a News

This chapter opens with a standard news article, then offers some variations commonly used by groups and organizations: an external newsletter article, an internal newsletter article, a news memo, and a report of a meeting.

FUMES FORCE EVACUATION OF ALLIED CAFETERIA

A company safety officer ordered the evacuation of the Allied Insurance Company cafeteria Wednesday afternoon when more than 30 patrons and several food workers complained of feeling sick. The cause is under investigation.

Three persons remained under observation at area hospitals last night. The rest were treated on site by the Oldtown emergency rescue squad and released.

Allied's chief environmental safety officer, Karen Oliver, called in the emergency rescue squad at 2:11 p.m. after learning from cafeteria manager Gary Barbary that one food worker had collapsed and two others were feeling dizzy.

When Oliver arrived at the cafeteria five minutes later, other workers and a number of patrons were complaining of symptoms ranging from nausea and shortness of breath to faintness and blurred vision.

Oliver ordered the immediate evacuation of the cafeteria and told Barbary to shut down all kitchen equipment. Rescue workers, who arrived at about 2:25 p.m., moved workers and patrons with severe symptoms to a nearby conference room for emergency treatment.

Oliver also called in inspectors from the state Office of Environmental Health. They began air quality testing shortly after 3:00 p.m., but the results were inconclusive. OEH plans to conduct more thorough tests for the next several evenings when most employees are out of the building.

"The symptoms suggest carbon monoxide to me," said OEH inspector Christina Medaglio. "The ventilation system is twenty years old and may not be adequate to handle the output from the additional cooking equipment installed last summer."

Allied vice president Walter Williams said that the ventilation system and older cooking equipment, both of which date from the late 1960s, had passed a state inspection last June.

Williams said that since the cafeteria has its own separate ventilation system, the fumes posed no threat to workers in other parts of the six-story building.

OEH has ordered that the cafeteria remain closed until further notice.

News Article Format

This classic news story reports an event in standard journalistic style and could appear in a local newspaper, a company newsletter, or a news release sent to a local newspaper. (See Chapter 4 for more on press releases of all kinds.)

LEAD The 33-word first paragraph summarizes the story, covering *who* (the safety officer, workers, and patrons), *what* (evacuating the cafeteria), *where* (Allied Insurance Company), *when* (Wednesday afternoon), and *why* (complaints of feeling sick). NOTE: *Those five are the standard questions any reporter must discover by first-hand observation or by interviewing those at the scene. The answers to those questions go in the story's lead.*

BODY As in all classic news stories, the body of this article follows inverted pyramid order, placing the most important and most current information first and delaying background and history till later.

The paragraphs in news stories are only one to three sentences long, giving the narrow columns of newsprint a more open, less crowded feeling. In Sample 9, each paragraph makes a separate point. Paragraph 2 answers the question raised by the lead about what happened to the patrons and workers who became ill. Paragraphs 3–6 return to the beginning of the story and offer a detailed narration of the afternoon's events in chronological order. The next two paragraphs address questions about the source of the fumes and the age of the equipment, pinning down the details with testimony from both the OEH inspector and the Allied vice president.

CONCLUSION The final two paragraphs offer information related to the ongoing safety of Allied workers and the status of the cafeteria. The focus on "what's next" rounds the article off.

Writing News Stories

A news story informs readers about something that has happened recently, is happening currently, or will happen in the near future. It is reported in a neutral tone and generally follows inverted pyramid order. It concentrates on factual information, sometimes using quotations to convey the opinions of key people, but it never expresses the writer's opinion or analysis and never uses the first person ("I") except in quotations.

INVERTED PYRAMID ORDER In inverted pyramid order the most important part of the story comes first (the fat end of the pyramid), the least important details come last (the narrow end of the pyramid), and the other information is presented in descending order of importance in between. Inverted pyramid order, or a slight variation on it, is the most common way to organize a news story for two reasons. First, it allows readers to scan the opening sentences of each news story to decide whether or not to read further. Second, it allows a newspaper or newsletter editor to cut from the bottom of a story, knowing that essential information will not be left out.

LEADS The lead is the opening of a news or feature story. The classic lead is a summary that covers, in 30 to 40 words, all or most of the Five W's and an H—**who, what, where, when, why,** and **how**—of the story.

Some leads immediately identify specific names, dates, and locations. This approach works well when readers are likely to recognize or be interested in the specifics because of fame, familiarity, or timeliness. Other leads give only a general summary in their first paragraph and defer specifics to following paragraphs. This approach is advisable when the impact of what happened might get lost in the details. Some journalists suggest that this approach is most appropriate when what happened is more interesting than who it happened to, where and when it happened, and so forth.

Compare these two summary leads:

1. Jane Adder, a junior at Oldtown High School, captured the gold medal in the International Science Olympics in Uppsala, Sweden, yesterday, defeating semifinalists from Japan and Canada.

2. A state high school junior captured the gold medal in the International Science Olympics in Uppsala, Sweden, yesterday, defeating semifinalists from Japan and Canada.

The first lead would work well in an Oldtown newspaper or in the high-school newsletter because readers of both are likely to recognize the name of the high school or that of the student herself. The second lead is more suitable for a newspaper in another part of the state or for the newsletter of a regional teachers' organization. For these readers, the fact that a state student won is more important than her name or her school, details that would come in the second paragraph.

BODY The body, following inverted pyramid order, treats the most important people, events, or issues of the story first. In a news story, most important means most newsworthy, most

THE FIVE W'S AND AN H

WHO The individual, organization or group, city, state, or country that plays the lead role in the story.

WHAT What happened, the event the story is about. While the *what* is the main focus of most leads, sometimes the *who* or the *where* or the *when* may be of more interest. For example, working out in the company gym is not in itself a remarkable action, but if the governor drops in to use the Nautilus machine, it's news. A hundred people taking a swim at a Chicago beach is news only when it occurs on New Year's Day.

WHERE The story's location. The *where* may be as specific as a room or an address, as general as a state or country. In an internal newsletter or memo, the place of a regular meeting may simply be the name of a well-known room (e.g., Hill Laboratory). But an external newsletter article might specify the building and floor (Hill Science Laboratory, on the fifth floor of Reimann Hall).

WHEN The time, day, or date of the event being reported. In a daily newspaper article or press release, where a story isn't news unless it is fresh, time references should be as specific and recent as possible. Use *yesterday* or *tomorrow* or name the day of the week if the story is within seven days before or after the event; give the date (but not the day of the week) for events beyond this range. In a memo or announcement, giving the date in the heading may sometimes substitute for a time reference in the lead. In a newsletter published once or twice a month and thus read days or weeks after an event, time references may be more general (*last week, recently*).

WHY The cause or motivation for the main action the story describes. Depending on the story, the *why* may be the focus (as in a story on a fire department investigation of a chemical fire) or far on the periphery (as in a story about a new art exhibit, where presumably the reason for the exhibit is that the gallery likes the artwork and wants to showcase it).

HOW The way the event being reported came about. Again, in some stories this may be important enough to state in the lead (for example, the process by which a workforce reduction will be carried out), while in others it may be of much less interest, as in Sample 10, where the way the grant proposal was developed is deferred to the middle paragraphs.

31

timely. What's new is what's news. In Sample 11, p. 34, what's new is the action taken at the meeting. The background information on how the problem developed comes later.

Essentially, reporters and newspapers assume that readers want to know the latest developments first, that they want the bottom line to be the top line. Those who want further background or history can read on.

CONCLUSION Many news stories lack a conclusion, simply dwindling down to the less crucial or less interesting details. But it is also common to round off the story in the final paragraph, perhaps with a quotation that sums up the point of the story or with a look ahead to the consequences or the next step.

NEUTRALITY IN NEWSWRITING The news writer's stance should always be that of a reporter of information, not an analyst or evaluator or partisan. This means, for example, that reporters never use the first person "I" in news writing, that they avoid judgmental or suggestive language, that they do not take sides, and that they try to present the action or issue they are covering in a fair and balanced manner. In newspaper practice, this often means getting a statement from both sides on a controversial issue and reporting both neutrally. (For example, when police have named a suspect, good reporters not only get a statement from the police; they also get a statement from the suspect's lawyer. For most papers, balance is the quickest and most satisfactory method of appearing fair.)

ACCURACY Editors or supervisors require accurate information. This means checking and rechecking statistics and figures, dates and names (their exact spellings, along with preferences in nicknames, titles, and initials)—in other words, all the factual information in the story.

News stories must also report quotations accurately. Journalistic handling of oral quotations (unlike academic practice) allows reporters to juxtapose statements that were not made sequentially or to leave out words without using ellipsis dots, so long as these changes do not distort the context or intent of the speaker in any way. It is also common to clean up a speaker's unintentional errors, unless these errors reveal the speaker's characteristic style or views. For example, a quote from a speaker who, because of a pause for thought, said "the reasons . . . was" should be edited to read "the reasons were." But a quote from a speaker proclaiming opposition to feminism should not have uses of "he" to stand for both sexes changed to avoid sexist reference. The best rule is to edit only minor slips.

This article follows inverted pyramid order, with a 29-word lead covering *who* (the Office of Economic Development), *what* (awarding the grant), *where* (the cities and towns the grant will affect), and *why* (to increase business development in the Latino community).

HISPANIC INSTITUTE RECEIVES $25,000 STATE GRANT

The Edgewood Park Hispanic Institute has received a $25,000 grant from the state's Office of Economic Development to increase Latino business development in cities and towns in eastern Texas.

States story's most important details concisely

The award, announced February 15, enables the Hispanic Institute to form a Latino Economic Development Center (LEDC) that will work with local Chambers of Commerce and merchants' groups both to stimulate the creation of new Latino-owned businesses and to provide technical assistance to existing Latino-owned firms.

Elaborates on lead, specifying when award was made and explaining how center will stimulate development

"The new economic development center offers the promise of the American dream to Latinos," said state OED secretary Marta Boucher in her announcement of the grant.

Uses quote to establish significance of grant

The proposal was the brainchild of the Institute's Gaspar Martinez, who worked with staffers Alicia Mercado and Ruben Alvarez to prepare it for submission to the OED last March. Martinez first became interested in Latino business development while doing the research for his doctoral thesis at Upstate University. When he joined the Hispanic Institute three years ago, his work with Oldtown Latino citizens' groups confirmed his sense of the urgency of revitalizing Latino neighborhood business areas. "I wanted to extend a hand to struggling business owners," Martinez says, "but my hand was empty. The Institute's funds were already committed, so I knew we had to look elsewhere."

Moves back to trace development of grant proposal

The state legislature had just passed a bill to provide for public-private cooperative funding of business development in economically distressed areas, and Martinez decided to apply for a grant. After three months of work with Mercado and Alvarez, Martinez submitted the proposal last October. He received news of the award in a phone call from Boucher on February 12.

Boucher expects funds to be available by July 1, and Martinez hopes to have the Latino Economic Development Center staffed and in operation by September 1.

Looks ahead to how grant will be implemented

33

This report of a union dispute, aimed at an internal audience, refers to the company by a shortened name and places in a later paragraph background information that should be familiar to most readers. Its 33-word lead tells *who* (the Classified Staff Union), *what* (the vote to refuse to negotiate), *where* (at the meeting), *when* (January 5), and *why* (the unmet demand for a new meeting place).

UNION DEMANDS REMAIN UNMET

States story's focus succinctly

The Classified Staff Union voted at its January 5 meeting to refuse to take part in further workload negotiations with Amalgamated management until the union demand for an adequate meeting room is satisfied.

Elaborates on current news: what happened at the meeting

Union members stood in the aisles and spilled out the doors of the Lewis Room during the 35-minute meeting. Nearly half of the attendees were unable to find seats.

"Management wants to keep our meetings small, so we won't give them any trouble," CSU president Sylvia Tasker said in presenting the motion from the executive committee. "But the smaller they try to keep us, the more trouble we'll give them." Her attempts to call for discussion of the motion were drowned out by cheers for several minutes. After a brief discussion, the motion passed by a nearly unanimous voice vote.

Explains how the problem developed. Presents management's side through the Wheeler quote to add sense of impartiality

An increase in hiring and a membership drive by CSU have increased union membership by almost 40 percent since September, bringing its current size to 307. In October, Tasker requested permission to move meetings from the 125-seat Lewis Room to the 300-seat Amalgamated auditorium. Vice President Michael Wheeler denied the request. "We need to keep the auditorium open for lectures and presentations to the public, " Wheeler said in his written response to Tasker, adding that attendance at union meetings had typically been less than 50 percent of the membership.

Returns to the recent meeting and elaborates union position. While writer does not seem to take sides, paraphrased argument from Yeoman and January 5 attendance figure may influence readers to see logic of union position

But in the discussion of the motion, CSU secretary Sam Yeoman pointed out that regular lectures occur only on Wednesday and Thursday evenings, while the union regularly meets on Tuesdays. Tasker's October request stated that the union would be willing to work out any schedule conflicts. Official attendance at the January 5 meeting was 237.

"They want us to pitch in and take on extra hours because of the big federal contract," Tasker said after the meeting. "But they're not willing to budge on this. So no space, no negotiation."

The union's executive committee meets Tuesday, January 12, to consider further strategy.

This memo is organized exactly as a news article would be, though the names of the two unions and their presidents and the date are given only in the opening headings. Like a news lead, the opening paragraph covers *who* (classified staff), *what* (the choice of holidays), *where* (at Amalgamated), and *how* (through negotiations), with *when* (in the future) implicit in "may choose."

FROM: Sylvia Tasker, President, Classified Staff
           Union
           Agnes Middleton, President, Professional
           Staff Union
TO: Amalgamated Classified and Professional
           Staff
DATE: October 20, 1996
SUBJECT: November holiday options

As a result of negotiations between our two unions and management, Amalgamated classified and professional staff may choose either to take off the November 11 Veterans' Day holiday or to work that day and take off the Friday after Thanksgiving.

All employees will soon receive a form for indicating their choice. This form must be filed with the Personnel Office no later than noon, November 1. All Amalgamated divisions will be in operation both days, though some staff may be assigned to work outside their division for that day only. Any employee who does not complete the form must take off the November 11 holiday and work on the day after Thanksgiving.

Offers essential and current information about what employees must do and how the company will operate on the holiday

In past years, the Friday after Thanksgiving was a regular workday at Amalgamated, and employees who wanted to take it off had to count it as a vacation day. In early September, 56 classified staff members submitted a petition asking for the chance to choose between the November 11 holiday and the day after Thanksgiving. Following approval of a motion supporting this petition at the September 15 CSU meeting and passage of a similar motion at the September 22 PSU meeting, negotiators from both unions met with management representatives in early October.

Offers less crucial information about the history of the holidays and the request for policy change

After consulting with division heads and the personnel office, management representatives agreed to the proposal on a trial basis for this year. Union and management representatives will meet in early December to evaluate this year's trial and to explore the possibility of a permanent policy offering this choice.

Returns to the present and looks to the future

35

As you can see by comparing this article to the minutes of the meeting (Sample 49, p. 144), this story does not follow the order of items on the meeting's agenda. Instead, it treats the most newsworthy decision of the commission first, in accordance with inverted pyramid order; then it summarizes other items in decreasing order of importance or newsworthiness.

SENIOR CITIZENS COMMISSION
OPPOSES ELDERBUS CUTBACK

Focuses exclusively on most newsworthy issue

At its January 18 meeting, the Hometown Senior Citizens Commission voted to oppose the curtailment of Elderbus service.

Elaborates by summarizing discussion at meeting and giving actual vote count. Note that it includes details of debate observed by writer but not reported in minutes (See Sample 49, page 144)

During the discussion of the motion, commission member Solomon Green called Mayor Barker's recent proposal to reduce Elderbus service "an outrage to Hometown seniors." Another commission member, Ethel O'Brien, pointed out that the proposed schedule changes would prevent many seniors from attending weekly movies at the Senior Center as well as the summer concerts by the lake, both of which take place on Thursday evenings. The motion to oppose the cutback in service passed by a vote of 8 to 1.

Offers historical background for readers less familiar with issue

The mayor's office announced early in January that, because of cutbacks in state funding for senior services, the Elderbus would operate on a new schedule beginning April 1, eliminating all service on Thursday evenings and on Saturdays, and reducing late afternoon service on other days.

Treats fuel assistance program next in order of importance

Also on the agenda was a motion to urge the city's participation in the state fuel assistance program for seniors. Robert Frank, of the State Energy Office, explained that the program requires 30 percent city funding and provides up to $400 a year to each eligible senior. Commission member Grace Chaleur pointed to a study showing that the average fuel bill for seniors last year was over $600, so the state program would cover only two-thirds or less of most seniors' costs. After a lengthy debate, further discussion was postponed until the February meeting.

Treats less newsworthy items briefly as "other business"

In other business, the HSCC urged expansion of the city's free blood pressure and diabetes screening program and approved plans for the May Senior Services Fair.

2b Feature Stories

Many articles don't treat current news but instead explore an issue in depth, provide historical or conceptual background, tell a poignant story, or profile interesting people. These are features. They may appear in a newspaper, newsletter, press kit, or may serve in other ways as promotional materials.

Readers love features; reporters have mixed feelings about them. People in journalism distinguish between hard news—deadline stories—and soft news—features. Fame in journalism is associated with hard news reporting, but everyone admits that features help keep papers afloat.

Feature is an elastic term that covers a great variety of stories. This section shows two prominent types, the independent feature and the sidebar. For an example of another type of feature, the personality profile, see Sample 19 (p. 58), and for a feature-style press release, see Sample 29 (p. 74–75).

SECURITY'S MARCIA ELLIS INVESTS IN LITERACY

Stylishly dressed in a gray pin-striped suit, softly tailored cream silk blouse, and Italian leather pumps, investment counsellor Marcia Ellis waits at her desk for her 6:00 P.M. appointment.

The door opens and another African-American woman enters: tiny, in her fifties, wearing a maid's uniform.

"Good evening, Alice. How are you?" Marcia asks.

"Good evening, teacher," Alice grins shyly. "My body is weary, but my mind is hungry to read the word of the Lord," she says, extracting a brightly colored Bible from a well-worn canvas bag.

"It's the most important part of my day," Marcia Ellis says later, explaining why she stays after work three days a week to help Alice learn to read. Marcia is one of 17 Security Investments employees participating in a company-sponsored alliance with the Oldtown Literacy Volunteer Program.

Alice, who grew up on a hardscrabble farm in southern Alabama, never had time to learn to read because she was too busy taking care of her eight younger brothers and sisters after her mother died in childbirth. But two years ago Alice began attending a Bible-based Christian church and realized that she could not become a baptized member unless she learned to read.

Marcia, on the other hand, attended private schools in a middle-class northeastern suburb and graduated with a degree in secondary education from Academia College. Faced with a decreasing demand for teachers, Marcia entered Security's training program in 1989 and became a certified broker in 1991.

But the itch to teach was still there. One night two years ago Marcia saw a bus ad for the Oldtown Literacy Volunteers Program and she signed up. Her first student was Alice, a domestic at a Suburbia apartment less than half a mile from Security. Marcia thought there must be a way for both of them to avoid the 45-minute commute to the OLVP office for their meeting, so she got permission from her supervisor, Al Clemens, to meet Alice at her office after hours.

Soon some of Alice's friends who also do domestic work asked her how they could sign up for reading and writing classes, and at about the same time, several of Marcia's co-workers began expressing interest in becoming literacy volunteers.

Marcia approached Security vice president Doris Lebowitz about finding space at Security for OLVP staff to offer tutor training sessions. Lebowitz readily agreed, even offering Security employees release time to attend these sessions. Now 17 Security employees work as literacy volunteers.

As the session ends, Alice has just finished Chapter 22 of the Book of Genesis. "Marcia let me run 15 minutes over," she says. "We couldn't stop with Abraham about to put the knife into Isaac, so we read till the Lord showed his mercy."

"Fifteen minutes is pretty little time to save a life," Marcia smiles.

"Two lives," Alice replies, "Isaac's and mine."

Feature Article Format

This feature article could appear in an internal or external newsletter, could be part of a press kit on Security's role in the community, or could be used in a variety of other ways as good publicity for Security.

LEAD Unlike the condensed summary leads typical of news stories, this lead uses five paragraphs to get to the main topic—the alliance between Security and the Oldtown Literacy Volunteer Program.

BODY Instead of inverted pyramid order, the writer uses chronological narration to develop the article. The narrative of the tutoring session, which begins in the lead and is taken up again at the end, frames the brief narrative of Alice's life and the longer narrative of Marcia's background and her role in getting Security to sponsor the OLVP.

CONCLUSION The last two paragraphs pick up the thread of the lead and bring the narrative of the tutoring session to a close with Alice's poignant punch line.

STYLE Unlike the neutral style of newswriting, this article spends time describing visual details and uses colorful, affective language like "stylishly," "shabby," "hardscrabble," and "itch to teach."

While the writer's voice never intrudes directly, details and a careful choice of quotations give readers the illusion of being there at the tutoring session and getting to know Alice and Marcia quite well. Most features are driven by personality, and this piece has the attention to detail that helps bring Marcia and Alice to life.

Writing Feature Articles

Feature is a broad term used to describe a wide range of articles that are not hard news and that do not need to be reported factually and impartially. Unlike news stories, features can look at the personal side of a story, can offer analysis or an in-depth look at an issue. They can also use colorful language and offer detailed descriptions, and they need not follow inverted pyramid order.

TYPES OF FEATURES There are two basic categories of features. What we will call the independent feature stands on its own. It may focus on a subject that is not hard news: an interesting person, a trend in education, a heartwarming story of kindness, a humorous episode. Or it may present news from a feature slant or angle. For example, when a New England power plant's cooling system began sucking in lobsters and one worker was found to have stashed away about 500 in his home freezers, Boston media covered the story humorously as "Lobstergate."

Another common type of feature, the sidebar, always accompanies a news story (the mainbar) and adds depth, background, or human interest. For example, with a news story of a corporate executive charged with bribing a public official, sidebars might include an in-depth analysis of the ethics of modern business, a personality profile of the executive, or a background story on the public official's past brushes with the law.

HOW FEATURES DIFFER FROM NEWS Features are less likely than news articles to follow inverted pyramid order. News puts the bottom line at the top in a summary lead, then treats information in decreasing order of importance. What grabs the reader's attention is the currency of the information in the story and the topic itself.

Features appeal to a less hurried reader, one willing to be wooed by a good story, or an unusual slant or insight. So a feature lead has to work harder to grab readers' attention, hooking them in by withholding crucial details or information till later in the article. The body of a feature can use narrative or other organizational plans to build the article up to its climax. And features always have conclusions, whether a simple wrap up or a long-awaited punch line.

FEATURE LEADS Because the lead in a feature must work hard to create interest in the reader, features use a much wider variety of leads than news stories commonly do. Here is a sampling of the approaches you can take in a feature lead:

- *Tell a story* A narrative lead, like the one in Sample 14, can intrigue readers and make them want to know what comes next or what the punch line will be. Narrative leads should be short enough so readers don't wonder what the point is halfway through, but long enough to make them feel involved.

- *Use a quote* A quotation lead can work when someone in the story has said something catchy or provocative or unintentionally ironic. Here's a good example—

> "I just wanted to see if it worked," said twelve-year-old Steve Archer as he surveyed the 6-foot hole in his family's garage made by his homemade laser gun.

Be warned, though, that quotations from well-known writers can be overworked. When you're tempted to run to your Bartlett's for a swell quote, the best advice is probably not to. If you must, give the quote a twist.

> "What is so rare as a sleigh in June?" Duluth residents asked themselves yesterday as they stared in amazement at the 2 inches of snow a freak storm dumped on their tomato plants, petunias, and marigolds.

- *Make a list* A staccato list can be a real attention getter, bombarding readers with images that add up to . . . what? It's not for every feature, but it can be fun.

> Bicycles. Tank tops. Sandals. Convertibles with their tops down. Combat boots. Flannel shirts. Fur coats. A typical July day in Harvard Square.

- *Set up a contrast* A contrast lead can highlight a dramatic change or can zero in on the unexpected. The list lead above plays on the contrast between the summer images and the increasingly incongruous additions to the list. Here's another:

> On May 1, 1991, Central Street between Vine and West was a dismal three-block stretch of massage parlors, pawn shops, and porno dealers, interspersed with boarded-up storefronts. On May 1, 1994, families strolled down the Central Crossing pedestrian mall, stopping at the candy store, the newsstand, or the old fashioned ice cream parlor. For Harborside residents, it was a dream come true.

- *Ask a question* A question lead can immediately engage readers. If the answer is unexpected, so much the better—

> What are the most common names for dogs today? If you answered Spot, Rover, and Lassie, guess again. A recent survey . . .

STYLE AND TONE Departing from the neutrality and detachment of news stories, features use descriptive, affective language to convey moods, feelings, implications—not just facts. Occasionally, a feature based on personal experience may even be written in the first-person "I" point of view.

This could appear next to the article in Sample 9 on p. 28, as background for the incident at the Allied cafeteria.

CAFETERIA INCIDENT RECALLS ALLEGATIONS AGAINST AIRFLO

Connects recent news to history

Wednesday's evacuation of the Allied Insurance cafeteria is the latest in a series of potentially hazardous incidents involving ventilation systems installed by Airflo Systems in buildings owned or formerly owned by the state.

Presents information in chronological order, as appropriate to sidebar giving historical context

In the 1980s, Airflo was low bidder on over 80 percent of all contracts for buildings constructed or renovated by the state. This included four of the five buildings in the Downtown Campus of the State University and the Department of Social Services building on Washington Street, which was sold to Allied Insurance in 1991.

As early as 1983, the *Oldtown Gazette* reported a possible conflict of interest in the awarding of low-bid contracts for state buildings. Then-senator William Roberts, chair of the legislature's Public Facilities Committee, which reviews bids for public buildings, was a major investor in HVAC, Inc., the parent company of Airflo. Roberts claimed that the investments had been made by his broker and that he was unaware of the alleged conflict of interest.

In 1987, a cafeteria on the Downtown Campus had to be evacuated because of complaints similar to those at the Allied cafeteria yesterday. A year later, students working in chemistry labs there were overcome by fumes.

State inspectors in both cases were unable to determine a cause, but an independent inspection team hired by the Office of Environmental Health issued a 1989 report finding that ventilation systems installed by Airflo in both buildings "substantially violated building codes and failed to comply with construction specifications."

Gives impression of impartiality by quoting Olafson

Airflo's troubles continued when a group of state employees working in the DSS building brought a class action suit against the company, citing an unusually high incidence of emphysema, asthma, and lung cancer among workers in the building. The case was settled out of court by HVAC, Inc. Henry Olafson, director of public relations for Airflo, claims that the company has records and invoices to prove that it constructed all systems in the state buildings according to contract specifications. "If there's a problem, it's with the specifications, not with our construction," Olafson said. "Airflo does first-rate work."

Returns to present investigation

Officials from OEH are conducting a full inspection of the Allied cafeteria ventilation system.

2c Some Notes on Journalistic Style

The principles of good journalistic style apply in most of the writing you'll do for a business, group, or organization. Here are some of the basics.

FOCUS ON THE MAIN CHARACTER Put the main actor(s) in the spotlight or "head" position in the sentence, as the subject of the first verb. Who are the main actors? That is for you to decide. Notice how the main actor differs in these two leads:

> A car struck and killed an elderly Oldtown woman as she crossed the street to attend Mass on Monday morning.

> An elderly Oldtown woman died when a car struck her as she crossed the street to attend Mass on Monday morning.

The first version puts the spotlight on the car, the second, on the victim. Unless the car or its driver is of special interest ("A car driven by an aide of Mayor Smith . . ."), the victim would usually come first in such a news story.

USE DYNAMIC VERBS Verbs like "was," "took place," and "happened" can make your sentences dull. And editors often caution against using passive-voice verbs—verbs like "were elected" and "was killed" in which the subject receives rather than performs the action. Whenever possible, substitute active verbs like "won the election" or "died." Notice the difference between the two sentences below:

> Paula Sands was elected to the City Council at its annual meeting last Tuesday.

> Paula Sands won a seat on the City Council at its annual meeting last Tuesday.

A dull account of a fire might say "The fire burned. . . ." To help think of dynamic verbs, visualize what happened: "Fire ripped through . . ." or "Flames destroyed . . ." or "A midnight blaze roared. . . ." Tabloids thrive on this highly charged language, so be aware that it's easy to overdo it once you get into the mood. But lively verbs have always been at the heart of journalistic writing. People don't always *sit*; they *ease* themselves into a chair or *perch on the edge* of a sofa or *settle comfortably* into an armchair. Prose like this makes feature writing come alive, and it has a place in straight news stories as well.

Some Notes on Journalistic Style

BE CONCISE Pack sentences with information, avoiding empty words like "there is" and overuse of connecting words like "which," "of," and "with." Compare the slow, wordy first passage below with the concise, lively revision that follows:

> There was a 12-year-old boy present who had studied CPR in one of the classes which he took to earn a Boy Scout merit badge; his name was Jason Wright. He asked the child's parents if he could help, and when they said yes, he knelt down beside the baby, who was unconscious, and began to do mouth-to-mouth resuscitation.

> Twelve-year-old Jason Wright, who had studied CPR to earn a Boy Scout merit badge, offered to help. With the parents' permission, he administered mouth-to-mouth resuscitation to the unconscious baby.

SAMPLE 16: FIVE LEADS FOR THE SAME STORY

Covers essential information but is drawn-out and spiritless; uses too many empty words like "of," "which," "who," and the colorless verb "was"	Last Friday, there was a theft of computer equipment which was worth $50,000 from the office of John Hunter, who is the Personnel Director of Data Systems.
Uses lively verbs—"broke into" and "stole"—but gives head position to shadowy "person or persons;" use "thieves"	An unknown person or persons broke into the office of Data Systems Personnel Director John Hunter on Friday and stole $50,000 worth of computer equipment.
Uses only moderately interesting verb—"are investigating"; spotlights police, who should not be main actors till next day's follow-up story on how investigation is proceeding.	The Oldtown police are investigating Friday's theft of $50,000 worth of computer equipment from the office of Data Systems Personnel Director John Hunter.
Spotlights John Hunter; article appropriate for internal newsletter, where readers might know him, or for sidebar on crime victims	Returning from a meeting Friday afternoon, Data Systems Personnel Director John Hunter found his office door jimmied open and $50,000 worth of computer equipment missing.
Uses passive verb ("was stolen") but highlights missing equipment, as readers of local newspaper might be more interested in goods stolen than corporate victim	Computer equipment worth $50,000 was stolen last Friday from the office of Data Systems Personnel Director John Hunter.

SHOW, DON'T TELL Compare these two sentences:

> The heavy elderly woman looked nervous and uncomfortable as she sat on the witness stand, listening to the lawyer's question.

> The woman shifted her bulk in the witness chair, her age-spotted hands shredding a tissue as she listened to the lawyer's question.

The second sentence gives readers the evidence, letting them witness the woman's discomfort. The first, offering no evidence, simply gives the writer's assessment. (At the same time, when readers need a generalization, go ahead and tell. There's no virtue in scattered details.)

KEEP PARAGRAPHS SHORT Newspaper and newsletter columns are narrow; a hundred words can take up three to four inches. Readers find paragraphs longer than that difficult to follow.

3

Interviews, Biographical Sketches, and Obituaries

The personal stories of group or organization members may take many forms: the employee-of-the-month interview in a staff newsletter, the profile interview of a new vice president in an external newsletter or press release, the speech honoring an award recipient, or the announcement of a colleague's death.

This chapter focuses on three common types of personal stories: the interview, the biographical sketch, and the obituary.

3a Interviews

The profile or personality interview is a common type of personal story in business speeches or publications and one of the most useful to master. It's the kind of article that appears in an in-house or external newsletter or that may be sent as a press release or as part of a press kit to introduce or showcase a staff member, guest speaker, or performer. (For more information on press releases and press kits, see pp. 69–79.)

The profile or personality interview takes two common forms. The feature article format (Sample 17) uses summaries, paraphrases, and well-chosen quotations to convey the content of the interview. The question-and-answer (Q-and-A) format (Sample 18) attempts to capture the exchange between interviewer and subject directly, without a narrator. We explain both formats below. Whichever you choose, basic journalistic principles should guide the way you organize information.

DR. SAMSON SEES NEW GOALS FOR FOUNDATION

Dr. Helene Samson wants the Medical Foundation to take the lead in forming a new alliance between medicine and politics in Georgia.

Dr. Samson, unanimously elected director of the Medical Foundation at the March 18 annual board meeting, acknowledges that she is proposing a major change in direction for the sixty-year-old foundation, whose primary focus has always been supporting medical research on diseases of the poor. Now Samson wants the foundation to work with state lawmakers to draw up a long-range plan to address the state's medical and sociomedical problems.

"Research that has no effect on public policy is futile," Samson says. "Take the resurgence of tuberculosis among the homeless. Research has shown that new antibiotics are needed to wipe it out, and research has produced those drugs. Some legislatures have even approved funds for distributing the medicine. But there is no system for identifying and reaching the victims, no follow-up to ensure that the drugs are being taken on schedule. So the money and research are wasted."

As a first step, Samson plans to ask the board to fund two new positions for public policy experts who can guide the foundation's new proactive approach. "We're all trained in medicine or in raising funds for research. We need expertise in how to shape and change public policy."

But this shift would not mean cutting back the foundation's traditional research role. "Research is the backbone of the foundation's work," Samson says, "but we can't stop there."

Samson, whose three-year term begins July 1, received her medical degree from Upstate Medical College. Before joining the foundation, she was in private practice in immunology for twelve years. She served as medical adviser to the State Commission on Infectious Diseases from 1985 to 1989. She joined the foundation as a research project director in 1989, focusing on how substance abuse was affecting the immune systems of inner-city teenagers.

A resident of Urban City, Samson is married to Dr. Michael Bush, a political science professor at State University. They have a son who will graduate this spring from Southeastern College with a degree in graphic arts and a daughter who will enter a pre-med program at Western University next fall.

Interview in Feature Article Format

Sample 17 would be suitable for an internal staff newsletter or for an external newsletter distributed to readers familiar with the work of the foundation.

HEADLINE The headline highlights the focus of the interview or the most interesting aspect of the interviewee's story.

LEAD The lead takes a news approach, giving readers a vivid capsule view of the interviewee. (It could also have taken any one of the approaches suggested in the feature leads section on pp. 40–41.)

BODY The body in Sample 17 follows inverted pyramid order, putting the most interesting and pertinent information first and working down to the more routine details (see pp. 29–30 for more on the inverted pyramid). (If what happened in the past had been crucial to the article's focus, then chronological order might have been more appropriate. In most cases, feature interviews put what is of current interest first and leave background till later.)

QUOTATIONS Sample 17 uses quotations to convey the interviewee's opinions on important issues, in this case the foundation's new goals. (Quotations are also used to reveal characteristic attitudes or phrasing, or to pull ideas together in especially effective ways.) The writer has paraphrased or summarized purely factual information and some opinions to avoid making the interview simply a patchwork of quotations. The interviewee is always clearly identified as the speaker of a quotation, either by using a phrase like "Samson says" or by using a sentence in the same paragraph to introduce the quotation (as in the fourth paragraph).

PARAGRAPHS Paragraphs here are short, as in newspaper style, for easy reading.

NOTE: *This interview could easily be adapted for a press release or an article in a newsletter with wider circulation by ending it with a "boilerplate" paragraph about the foundation, such as:*

Formed in 1934 to address the need for medical research on diseases of the poor during the Great Depression, the Medical Foun-

dation currently conducts research on the medical needs of the homeless and of recent immigrant populations in the greater Old-town area. The foundation is affiliated with the Ivy University Hospital and the Upstate Medical Center, and its board of directors includes some of the most prominent members of the local medical profession.

Writing the Interview

Whether you choose feature or Q-and-A format, the first paragraph or the opening question and answer, like the lead in any feature story, should capture the reader's interest and hint at things to come. Unless your focus is on your interviewee's past accomplishments, you should generally begin with something quite current and leave history until much later in the interview. The rest of the article may follow inverted pyramid order, chronological order, or another order appropriate to the nature of the interview. (See pp. 29–30 for more on inverted pyramid order and on leads and organizational patterns for feature articles.)

Feature article format, illustrated by Sample 17 (p. 48), relies mainly on summarizing and paraphrasing what you've learned from your interviewee and using well-chosen quotations to convey his or her personality, way of speaking, and strong views. For promotional profiles, it is safest to keep your tone formal and your voice impersonal. But for profiles in an in-house or less formal newsletter, especially those carrying your byline, more personal touches, such as descriptions of the setting of the interview and the physical appearance and gestures of the interviewee, may be appropriate.

The Q-and-A format may begin with a short summary of the interviewee's background and current situation, but this type of interview relies mainly on responses that have been edited to produce the illusion that the reader is actually participating in the conversation. To encourage this illusion, avoid using the first person ("I") in editing the questions for the published interview. Without that "I," readers can imagine that they are asking the questions and that the conversation is between them and the interviewee. The first person also distracts readers by focusing their attention on you rather than on the interviewee.

This is based on the same interview as Sample 17.

DR. SAMSON SEES NEW GOALS FOR FOUNDATION

Dr. Helene Samson, an immunologist, was unanimously elected director of the Medical Foundation at the board's March 18 meeting. She spoke to us recently about her agenda for change after she takes office on July 1.

Q. Why do the goals of the Medical Foundation need to change?
A. Fifty years ago the foundation was set up to help medical people get funds to support their research. But today research isn't enough. Medical problems have become social and political problems.

Q. Don't you find this situation overwhelming, even depressing?
A. No. It's a challenge. I see this as a unique opportunity to address the big issues of the 1990s and the twenty-first century, like AIDS and the current spread of tuberculosis among the homeless.

Q. You originally joined the Medical Foundation in 1989 as a researcher. What made you realize that research wasn't enough?
A. I was researching the effect of substance abuse on the immune system at that time, and it became clear to me that the medical issues could not be addressed without considering the economic and social conditions that fostered the problem. It's one thing to publish a report telling people that drug abuse among seventh graders has increased over 200 percent in the last three years. It's another thing to make legislators believe they have to fund programs to address this issue.

Q. Does this mean that the foundation should shift its focus from research to political lobbying?
A. No. What we need is to augment our research with the lobbying necessary to enact the solutions that our research points to. Research is crucial. It's the backbone of the foundation's work. But we can't stop there.

Q. How do you plan to put your agenda for the foundation into action?
A. I'll ask the board to fund two new positions for political or public policy experts who can guide the foundation's new active approach. On the present staff, we're all trained in medicine or in raising research funds. We need expertise in how to change public policy.

Provides context of Dr. Samson's election to presidency (If photo accompanies story, such information could appear in photo caption instead)

Arranges questions and answers in inverted pyramid order, using edited questions as topic headings

Uses "Q" and "A" and boldface type for questions to make it easier for readers to follow (A publication might replace "Q" with its initials, and "A" with initials of interviewee)

Omits quotation marks since format itself presents questions and answers as dialogue

Does not use "I" in edited questions

You have considerable freedom in editing such an interview: you may change the order of questions and answers, delete information from answers without indicating that you have done so, and combine information from the answers to several questions. Since the questions in a Q-and-A format function as topic headings, you may even invent questions that you didn't actually ask but that accurately represent the topic discussed and are appropriate to headline a part of your interviewee's response. But all this editing must produce a finished product that is true to the intent, spirit, and context of what your interviewee has said.

Conducting a Formal Interview

A formal interview involves an extended, in-person session in which you ask a series of prepared, well-researched questions. This type of interview is becoming somewhat less common, being replaced by easier, less intensive, more informal types of interaction. Briefer, less structured interviewing plays more and more of a role in researching and preparing articles, reports, or papers—the E-mail message to your friend the software engineer asking for technical information on computer fraud, the phone call to the company vice-president requesting a quote on the importance of a new product, the conversation in the hall with a co-worker to find out the ages of the employee-of-the-month's children. Still, the president of a university, the award-winning research scientist, the well-known writer on a publicity tour are all going to expect you to conduct a formal interview reflecting familiarity with their background and offering thoughtful and thought-provoking questions.

BEFORE THE INTERVIEW

- *Purpose* Make sure that you understand the purpose of the article you'll be writing. Is it to explore the subject's views on a particular topic? to introduce a new staff member or profile an upcoming guest speaker in an in-house publication? to get good press for your organization by showcasing a new director or by reviewing the accomplishments of a retiring staff member in a release sent to local media? to highlight the activities that made someone the employee-of-the-month or the recipient of some other award? Note that in these cases, as in almost all profile interviews written in organizational settings, the emphasis is on portraying the subject in a positive light. This has important implications for the tone you set throughout the conversation with your interviewee.

- *First contact* Contact with the interviewee or a member of his or her staff is usually initiated over the phone, well in advance. Unless you are interviewing someone on a promotional tour or someone seeking publicity for a book, a play, a political campaign, or a new product, you will probably need to establish some ground rules. Explain clearly your purpose and where the interview will appear. Find out how much time you will have. Ask if it is all right to tape record the interview.

- *Research* Good research is the key to a successful interview. Before you meet with your subject, get all the information you can. Interviewees will not be impressed if you have to ask for the correct spelling of their names or if you are unaware of their widely read book. Useful sources for background information include a resume or organizational biography, previously published interviews, phone calls to your subject's secretary or assistant or to people you know who are experts in the subject's field, and in some cases library reference tools like the international, American, and regional versions of *Who's Who* or specialized biographical works like *American Men and Women of Science, Contemporary Authors*, or *Who's Who in Finance and Industry*. If your interview will focus on issues as well as biography, your research should also include topics the interview is likely to cover, especially your subject's relevant recent publications and accomplishments.

- *Questions* Your research should help you generate a working list of both general and specific questions for the interview.
  - General questions ("What's it like being a dental surgeon?" "How would you address the state budget deficit?" "What can people do to become better writers?") have the advantage of allowing the interviewee to go in unexpected directions, opening up new avenues of questioning. They can also serve as warmups for more specific questions to come. But general questions can also be quite inhibiting to an inexperienced interviewee, who may feel put on the spot to make momentous pronouncements. You need to judge

both your subject and the moment in the interview to make the best use of general questions.

- Specific questions ("What do you do when a juvenile patient becomes hysterical in the dentist's chair?" "Why do you favor a hike in the alcohol and tobacco tax?" "At what point should a writer pay attention to grammar?") are the backbone of an interview because they are focused and relatively easy for your subject to respond to. But specific questions run the risk of being predictable and familiar to your subject so that the answers you get may also be predictable and rehearsed. One special risk involves closed-end questions ("Have you ever had a patient try to fight you off?" "Should taxes on alcohol and tobacco be raised?" "Is good grammar important?") because they're too easily answered with an unelaborated "yes" or "no." Closed-ended questions can be provocative—they're especially useful at helping pin down a verbose subject—but be prepared with follow-up questions if the response is brief.

DURING THE INTERVIEW

- *Setting the scene* The success of the interview depends heavily on how you present yourself and where the interview takes place, so follow these guidelines:
  - Dress appropriately. Take your cue from the way you expect your interviewee to dress. Showing up in jeans and T-shirt to interview a corporate executive or a political leader could appear disrespectful, while wearing a business suit to interview a grunge-rock guitar player would undermine your claim to be a follower of the scene.
  - Act pleasant and professional. Introduce yourself right away, stating your own position in the organization you represent and reminding your subject of the reason for the interview. Address the interviewee formally (Doctor Smith, Ms. Wilson, Professor Ames) unless invited to do otherwise.
  - Seek a suitable location. The wrong setting can make an interview difficult. Try to find a quiet, comfortable location where you and your interviewee can talk without interruption. A busy office where the phone rings frequently may disrupt the flow of your conversation. Close, cramped quarters may make your interviewee feel pressured; too great a distance may make both of you tense as you strain to hear

questions and responses. A noisy background may make a tape of the interview hard to understand. If the designated place seems unsuitable, politely ask whether it's possible to move to a quieter or less distracting location.

- *Asking the questions* If you've done your homework, you'll already have come up with some good questions. The next step is to decide how and when to use your questions so that both you and your subject are comfortable. The best profile interviews are conversations, not interrogations. So follow these practices of experienced interviewers:
  - Prioritize your list of questions in advance, keeping a compact list of the absolutely essential questions where you can easily refer to it.
  - Put your interviewee at ease. Start by thanking your interviewee for his or her time. Then try to establish some common ground, like being parents, struggling with a new company computer system, or surviving this morning's colossal traffic jam. Make your opening questions noncontroversial. ("Before you took this job, you lived in Santa Barbara. Are you finding it very different here?" "You last worked as development director for the Atlas Fund. What were some of your chief duties there?")
  - Use your list as a guide, not an agenda. Listen attentively and go with the flow. The more the interview turns into a conversation, the more successful it is likely to be.
  - Consult your list openly when you need to. Your interviewee expects you to have a list and to look at it from time to time. Being sneaky about it will distract both of you. So use your list openly to pick up the thread when there's a pause or to get the interview back on track.
  - Ask follow-up questions. Ask for more detail about interesting points or examples to pin down general statements; request more information about references you aren't familiar with or concepts that aren't clear to you; clarify spellings of names or technical terms. Don't be afraid to show your ignorance here.

- *Recording the interview* Should you tape the interview or just take notes? Your decision depends on three things: the format of the finished interview, the reaction of your interviewee, and your own preference.
  - Format of the finished interview: If you plan on writing your interview in the Q-and-A format (see Sample 18,

p. 51), taping it is your only option. Otherwise, the choice between taping and notetaking depends on your subject's preference and your own.

- Reaction of the interviewee: Taping is clearly inhibiting to some interviewees, particularly inexperienced ones. Always ask permission to tape an interview, but don't take a "yes" for a final answer. If you see that an interviewee is talking to the tape recorder instead of to you, stop taping and rely on notes. It's better to miss some words than to make your interviewee nervous and self-conscious.
- Your own preference: Do you like the freedom of letting the machine get things down while you keep the conversation going? Or are you nervous about the tape running out or the machine malfunctioning? If neither the format nor the interviewee's nervousness mandates a choice, go with what you are most comfortable with.

- *Some guidelines for effective taping and notetaking*
  - Taping: Bring more tapes than you think you'll need. Always test the recorder on site before relying on it for the interview—there's nothing worse than finding out that your softspoken interviewee's voice is all but inaudible because of where you placed the tape recorder during the interview. If you can, set a timer for several minutes before you expect your tape to run out so that you won't have to switch tapes during a crucial response. Finally, always take back-up notes; both tape recorders and their operators are fallible.
  - Notetaking: Take notes sparingly, jotting down key phrases rather than whole sentences. Rely on careful listening and your memory for larger contexts. Unless you are writing in the Q-and-A format (which necessitates taping the whole conversation), most of your interview will paraphrase what your subject tells you, using only a few colorful or characteristic quotations. Don't be shy about asking your interviewee to repeat a statement you'll probably want to quote. Say that you want to get it down just right. You can even reconstruct short quotes from key phrases jotted down, as long as you make sure that the gist and intent are accurate. If you're in doubt, verify quotations by phone before you go to print.

3b Biographical Sketches

A biographical sketch, sometimes called a "bio," may range from a feature-like overview of a person's achievements and interests to a narrowly focused account of selected aspects of a person's life and accomplishments. The profile or personality interview can be a kind of biographical sketch. But you are probably familiar with several other types:

- an internal newsletter profile of an employee-of-the-month
- a political campaign flier account of a candidate's background and experience
- a speech that later gets published highlighting the accomplishments of an award or prize recipient
- a theater program synopsis of cast and crew members' previous stage experience

While you may be asked to write an employee-of-the-month profile that has much in common with the personality interview, you may also be called upon to compose sketches that are briefer and narrower, tailored to a specific situation and audience. For example, biographical sketches are often an important element in publicity and public relations. A fund-raising campaign for a hospital may profile the credentials and accomplishments of some of its distinguished staff members as a way to impress potential donors. A press kit on a new high-tech product may bring human interest to a possibly dry topic by offering some insight into its developers.

Because of the variety of biographical sketches, this chapter offers five samples that range from a longer feature-style article to an award speech to a brief program note.

IN THE SPOTLIGHT: STEVE ATLAS

United Freight employee-of-the-month Steve Atlas, who will compete in the statewide Muscle Man contest August 1, has earned a reputation among his bosses and co-workers as the one to turn to when the going gets tough or, rather, when the lifting gets heavy.

Package handler Ed Farley recalls one day last week when the division was in a hurry to get out a shipment and all the fork lifts were in use. "I saw Steve pick up an air conditioner carton that must have weighed 250 pounds. He made it look like it was a box of ping-pong balls."

Steve's dependability matches his strength. He hasn't missed a day of work in his six years at United. "If you're strong, you'll stay healthy," Steve often advises his fellow workers, and he seems to be living proof of what he preaches.

But what really makes Steve such a valuable employee are his work ethic and his personality. "He never holds back or loafs on the job," says supervisor Amy Loventhal, who nominated him for employee-of-the-month. "In fact, he looks for opportunities to help others when we're between shipments. If we had two Steves, we'd probably run out of work about five times a day."

Yet Steve is universally liked by co-workers. "You'd think a workaholic like Steve would be a real pain," says package handler Marie Bastile. "But he never gets on anybody, and he tries to lend a hand if he sees you're tired or having a bad day. He always asks how you are and really listens to the answer. But he keeps working while he listens," she adds.

Steve grew up in Oldtown and attended Oldtown High, where he wasn't particularly athletic. But things changed when he enlisted in the Marine Corps right after graduation. "I got hooked on basic training," Steve says. "I'd still be in the Marines if I could do basic all the time, but they put me on maintenance work, and there was too much sitting around."

That was when Steve took up weightlifting. "It was almost as good as basic—just no mud or barbed wire," Steve says with a grin. When the opportunity came to work as a package handler, Steve thought it was the perfect job, "a good way to stay in shape and get paid for doing it."

Steve began competitive weightlifting about two years ago, winning the citywide competition last December and the Eastern Counties Regional in April. So what are his chances for a first place medal on August 1?

"My chief competition is a guy named Andy Kent who trains six hours a day. But, hey, I train eight hours a day at United and then go to the gym for three more hours. I gotta figure I got the edge," Steve says.

Format for Newsletter Article Biographical Sketch

This newsletter article, like many personality interviews, follows inverted pyramid order, aims at a fairly rounded picture of its subject, and includes quotations from the subject himself. But unlike a personality interview, this newsletter article includes quotes and information from co-workers and friends to show what Steve is like and why he deserves the employee-of-the-month award.

LEAD The lead in this in-house article is appropriately informal, humorously playing on the connection between Steve's job and his hobby.

BODY The body follows inverted pyramid order, placing the qualities that have made Steve employee-of-the-month first. The anecdote quoted from a co-worker dramatically illustrates Steve's physical strength on the job, his attendance record shows his reliability, and the quotations from Loventhal and Bastile show the personal traits that made him popular with co-workers.

History, which is less important to Steve's selection as employee-of-the-month, is not introduced till about two-thirds of the way into the article. Paragraphs 6 and 7 tell how Steve got into weightlifting and decided to work at United. The quotes show Steve's passion for physical training as well as his sense of humor.

CONCLUSION The last two paragraphs round off the article by looking to the upcoming competition and by ending with a characteristic and humorous quote from Steve.

STYLE The subject of the article is referred to throughout by his first name only, as is appropriate to this informal in-house publication. (But note—even in-house newsletters vary in level of formality. For example, a professional staff newsletter in a hospital may refer to doctors and nurses as Dr. Smith, Mr. Jones, etc.)

A bulleted or resume-style format like this can be suitable for promotional biographical materials.

WHAT SANDRA O'DONNELL CAN GIVE YOU IN THE STATE LEGISLATURE

EFFECTIVE LEADERSHIP

Lists accomplishments as elected city official first, with rest listed in descending order of importance

- Member of Oldtown City Council since 1988

  Chaired committee to streamline city fiscal policies
  Led effort to build a new main library
  Helped draft fair housing ordinance
  Co-chaired City Property Re-Use Committee

- Chair of Oldtown Democratic City Committee 1992–1994
- Treasurer of Oldtown Chamber of Commerce 1990–1992
- Copresident of Oldtown Middle School PTA 1991–1993

COMMITMENT TO ENVIRONMENT

Lists affiliations and activities generally in descending order of importance

- Elected to Board of Directors, Friends of Oldtown Harbor 1994
- Active member of Sierra Club since 1987
- Secretary, State Audubon Society 1982–1985
- Oldtown Recycling Committee member since 1983

BUSINESS AND MANAGEMENT EXPERTISE

Lists current store ownership first, followed by academic degree to establish professional credentials

- Owner/manager of Save Our Planet Emporium since 1984
- M.B.A., State University 1980
- Small business consultant 1980–present
- Oldtown Small Business Coalition 1995–present

PERSONAL AND COMMUNITY COMMITMENT

Serves as catch-all to highlight advocacy of community causes as well as to establish personal ties to community

- Advocate for neighborhoods, affordable housing, and education
- Board of Directors, Safe Haven, housing for battered women
- Lifelong resident of Oldtown
- Married, mother of three children in Oldtown Public Schools

I am pleased to announce on behalf of the board of directors that the Allied Systems Achievement Award for 1993 goes to chief systems engineer Elaine Howard of our educational systems division.

We honor Ms. Howard tonight for her invention and development of scientific educational software that has helped to make Allied a national leader in this field.

Ms. Howard, who holds a Ph.D. in systems design from the State Institute of Technology as well as an M.S. in environmental science from State University, joined Allied in 1987 as a systems engineer in the Educational Division. Over the next several years, she took the lead in developing self-instructional programs on ozone depletion and the rainforest ecosystem that have been adopted in more than 100 school systems nationwide.

In 1991, aided by a $100,000 grant from the Governor's Council on Technology in Education, Ms. Howard began work on the environmental game Liquid Assets, which uses interactive CD-ROM technology to help high school students learn about the pressures put on local water resources by industrialists and developers.

High school teachers feed information about an actual local watershed area into Liquid Assets' interactive CD-ROM program. Their students act out the roles of developers, industrialists, conservation commission members, city councillors, environmental activists, and state environmental officials. This innovative CD-ROM program provides information for students' reports and proposals, and predicts consequences of those decisions and actions.

Ms. Howard and her assistants Carol Kubumba and Manuel Alvarez worked closely with teachers at Oldtown High School and with the North River Watershed Association to develop a model program that was classroom tested at Oldtown High during the 1992–93 academic year. In the past six months, Liquid Assets has been recognized in *Newsmonth* magazine as one of the five best new approaches in science education, and Allied has received an award from the National Teachers Association for the development of this game.

Elaine Howard's creativity and technological innovation exemplify the spirit and image of Allied Systems. We are proud to recognize her achievement tonight.

Summary lead identifies speaker's role

Uses courtesy title "Ms."

Works educational background in unobtrusively, but includes no personal information

Details chronologically Howard's major contributions to Allied's Educational Division and national recognition of her work

Sums up Howard's contribution to Allied

SAMPLE 22: BRIEF BIOGRAPHICAL SKETCH FOR PUBLIC RELATIONS USE

This brief, neutral bio is typical of those kept in an organization's files for use in public relations and promotional contexts. It could be part of a press kit or could accompany an annual report, fund-raising mailings, or grant proposals.

Gives Ready's current title and summarizes his view on key issue

John Ready, Clinical Specialist for Family Therapy, has been with the Rehabilitation Institute since 1987. He sees the family as an integral part of the recovery process for RI's teenaged spinal-cord injury victims.

Refers to Ready formally by last name only, as newspaper would

In 1989, Ready took the lead in making RI one of the first programs in the country to institute mandatory family therapy for all patients. Ready is also responsible for educating and consulting with RI staff on helping patients and their families handle the depression and behavioral problems arising from the injury. He has published numerous articles in professional and popular journals on the disruptive effects of such injuries on families and was the first to call public attention to the 60 percent divorce rate among parents of spinal-cord injury victims.

Summarizes Ready's accomplishments at RI and in his field of research

Previously, Ready was in private practice in Mount Hill, specializing in counseling patients with physical disabilities. He has also worked with Tech Valley Corporation to develop an eye-controlled computer communication system for quadraplegics. Ready received his B.S. in psychology from Academic College and his Ph.D. in clinical psychology from Upstate University.

Ends with summary of previous employment and education

SAMPLE 23: BRIEF BIOGRAPHICAL SKETCH FOR THEATER PROGRAM

Brief, focused bios like this one might appear in a music-school or adult-education catalogue, in print materials accompanying an art exhibit or video festival, or in a brochure for a professional conference.

Follows education with summary of work for theater companies

ANDREA DIVA (Titania) is a graduate of the Drama Conservatory and the International School of Music. She has been acting and singing in the Oldtown area for the past five years, performing with the Masquerade Players, the Oldtown Opera, and the Intown Chamber Singers. Her roles have included Bianca in *Kiss Me Kate*, Buttercup in *H.M.S. Pinafore*, and Cressida in Shakespeare's *Troilus and Cressida*. Regulars at Proscenium performances will remember her as Domina in last season's production of *A Funny Thing Happened on the Way to the Forum*. Andrea also teaches drama and music at the Oldtown Middle School.

Lists previous roles, with special emphasis on recent Proscenium performance

Refers to actress by first name

3c Obituaries

An obituary is an announcement of someone's death and a summary of the accomplishments that made this person known within a city, town, community, or organization. While most obituaries in large newspapers are written by junior reporters, you may be called upon to write one about a member of your company or organization for publication in newspapers, professional or trade journals, alumni newsletters, in-house or external newsletters, or interoffice memos to staff.

This section first presents a basic newspaper obituary. Even if you are faced with filling out a typical newspaper's standard form, you'll find it helpful to know what information will be asked for. Next is a model of an expanded obituary suitable for a press release, professional journal, or newsletter. The third model offers a more personal announcement suitable for internal distribution to members of an organization or community.

MARIA GOMEZ, 44, TEACHER

Maria (Santos) Gomez, 44, a fifth-grade teacher at the Dewey Elementary School, died Sunday at her home in Oldtown after a lengthy battle with breast cancer.

Ms. Gomez was born in Pueblo Viejo, Puerto Rico, and moved to the Center City area at the age of 11. A 20-year resident of Oldtown, she graduated from St. Hugo's High School. She received a bachelor's degree in mathematics from City College and a doctorate in education from State University. In 1987, she joined the staff at Dewey Elementary School, where she taught fifth grade for six years until her illness forced her to take a leave of absence in the fall of 1994. She previously taught fourth grade at the Academy School.

She was active in the local Teachers Union, serving as its secretary from 1989 to 1991. From 1986 to 1993, she served on the board of directors of the Oldtown Community Development Corporation and chaired its committee on Hispanic Affairs.

An avid runner, Ms. Gomez completed the Oldtown Marathon seven times and placed among the top 200 runners in the senior women's division in 1993. She also served as a volunteer coach for the Oldtown High School cross-country team.

She leaves her husband, Carlos R.; a daughter, Carlotta, of Upstate, N.Y.; two sons, Miguel and Roberto, both of Oldtown; her parents, Carmen and Alonso Gomez, of Rio Claro, P.R.; and a sister, Elene Gaspar of Suburbia.

A funeral mass will be said at 10 A.M. on Wednesday at Holy Savior Church in Oldtown. Burial will be in the County Cemetery in Center City.

Memorial donations may be made to the Maria Gomez Performing Arts Fund, in care of the Dewey Elementary School.

Newspaper Obituary Format

Sample 24 is typical of a first day (or same day) obituary.

LEAD The lead includes Maria Gomez's full name, including her maiden name in parentheses; her age; her most recent job; and the day, place, and cause of her death.

NOTE: *If this were a second day obituary, the lead would focus on the funeral or memorial service rather than the death: "A funeral mass will be said at 10 A.M. tomorrow for Maria Gomez, a teacher at the Dewey Elementary School who died Sunday at her home in Oldtown after a lengthy battle with breast cancer. She was 44."*

BODY The body focuses first on Gomez's background and accomplishments, describing her education, her role in the Teachers Union and the Community Development Corporation, and her athletic pursuits. It then names her survivors, noting the city where each lives. It ends with funeral and burial arrangements.

Writing an Obituary

Obituaries are among the most formulaic of articles; they are what cub reporters traditionally cut their teeth on. Some newspapers use a form requesting all the relevant information and insist that the actual obituary be written by the staff. If your newspaper doesn't require a form, follow the pattern below.

LEAD The first paragraph of the obituary should include:
- the full name of the deceased. Give a nickname in quotation marks; place a woman's maiden name in parentheses before her married name.
- the place where the death occurred
- the city or town where the deceased most recently lived. For a nursing home resident, a college student, or someone on a temporary job assignment, the city or town where he or she formerly lived would also be listed.
- current or former position or other characterization to show how the deceased was known in the community
- the day on which the death occurred
- the cause of death. Some newspapers allow the phrase "long illness," while others require the exact cause of death. Sometimes just "cancer" is permitted; more often, papers want to know what type of cancer.
- age of the deceased

BODY The body of the obituary should include:
- the decedent's history and accomplishments, including diplomas, awards, affiliations, and memberships in athletic, volunteer, or civic organizations
- a list of survivors, giving the name of a spouse or companion, followed by those of children, parents, and siblings, and noting the city or town where each resides as well as the number of grandchildren and great-grandchildren. Most papers have their own rules about how detailed a list of survivors is permitted.
- details of funeral or memorial service and burial

The most common newspaper obituaries cover only the above information and maintain a neutral tone. However, newspaper obituaries for prominent people and newsletter or in-house obituaries can elaborate on that basic format and content in a number of ways. An expanded newspaper or newsletter obituary for a local politician may take on some characteristics of a feature article, quoting from previously published interviews with the deceased and from other politicians who knew the deceased well, and even recounting humorous or typical anecdotes from the decedent's life (see Sample 25 below). A newsletter article or a press release may also convey the collective regret of the issuing institution, corporation, or organization and may include quotations and anecdotes. A memo may express a very personal sense of loss on the part of a supervisor and may recall details of particular significance to the decedent's colleagues.

RESEARCHING AN OBITUARY In an institution, corporation, or organization, start with the personnel office. The decedent's resume and any biographical sketches on file will supply much of the information you need about education, previous employment, and awards. You may find further details in press releases, in-house newsletters, and standard biographical reference materials like those used for interviews (see p. 53).

It is important to have a clear sense of the kind of obituary you are being asked to write. For a basic newspaper obituary, you may find most or all of what you need in the files. But for a more extended newspaper obituary or for a newsletter article, press release, or memo you write for a supervisor, you will certainly need to consult the decedent's co-workers, supervisors, assistants, and even family members to get a fuller picture and appropriate quotations, memories, and anecdotes.

This obituary might be sent to the press by an employer's public relations staff or might appear in an external newsletter.

RONALD FRIENDLY, 55,
CHAIR—UNITED CHARITIES

Ronald Friendly, chair of the United Charities Fund and four-term state representative, died unexpectedly of pneumonia at Mercy Hospital on Thursday. He was 55.

Focuses on Friendly's best-known roles as United Charities Fund chair and state representative

As state representative, Mr. Friendly sponsored key legislation on women's rights and fair housing. But the accomplishment of which he was most proud was the Education Reform Act of 1987. "If we fail our children, we have lost the future," he said in an *Observer* interview following the passage of the acts.

Uses courtesy title "Mr." to show respect

He took over the chairmanship of United Charities in 1991, when the organization's credibility had been undermined by the indictment of its previous chairman on charges of embezzling United's funds. In the following three years, Mr. Friendly accomplished a turnaround of United's image that *Newsmonth* magazine called "nothing short of miraculous."

A devout churchgoer, Mr. Friendly was characterized by Helen Dubois, a member of United's Board of Directors, as "scrupulously honest and unfailingly fair." He was also famous for his deadpan humor. As Muriel Underling, head of United's public relations department, said yesterday, "He sometimes had fun pretending to be a curmudgeon, even imitating W. C. Fields. But the door to his office was always open, and it seemed as if no one went away without getting some help. He always seemed to find a way."

Quotes from United board member and employee to add personal dimension

Raised in Suburbia, Mr. Friendly graduated from Main State College, served three years in the Air Force, and received a doctorate in Economics from Duketon University. He taught economics at Adams College for six years and served as a political aide to Governor Smith before his successful run for state representative in 1982.

Defers details of Friendly's education and prior employment until late in the article

In recent years, he served on the Social Service Committee of New Covenant Lutheran Church. He occasionally acted in productions of the Amateur Thespians, most recently appearing as Scrooge in last December's production of *A Christmas Carol*.

Mentions community service and amateur acting to round out his role in community

He is survived by his wife, Catherine N. (McBride), his daughters, Mary and Angela, and his father, George R., all of Suburbia; and by his brother, Robert G. of Lakeville, Mississippi. A private funeral service will be held Saturday at Eternal Repose Cemetery in Easttown. Memorial contributions may be made to United Charities.

Gives funeral and memorial information last

SAMPLE 26: DEATH ANNOUNCEMENT TO COMMUNITY OR ORGANIZATION

Sent to parents of Dewey Elementary School students and former students by its principal, this article centers on lively and touching memories of the late teacher, combining the principal's personal recollections with those of colleagues.

NOTICE TO THE DEWEY SCHOOL COMMUNITY

Focuses first on expression of sadness and on memorial service, since many parents will already have heard of the death by word of mouth or from a newspaper

Refers to decedent familiarly as "Maria"

Offers lively and touching memories, combining personal recollections with those of Maria's colleagues

Gives information about fund for those who want to contribute

The faculty at Dewey Elementary School join me in expressing their deep sadness at the death of our colleague Maria Gomez. Maria died of breast cancer on Sunday, January 28.

We invite you and your children to join us and Maria's family and friends at a memorial service on Saturday, February 24, at 10 A.M. in the school auditorium.

Before she was forced to take a leave of absence last fall, Maria had taught fifth grade at Dewey for six years. All of us who worked with her knew her as a person who cared deeply for each of her students and who tackled problems with unfailing patience.

When Maria was first diagnosed with cancer in 1994, she faced the challenge with courage and humor, using the opportunity to educate her students about the disease and the effects of chemotherapy. No one who was with us that year will forget her "Design-a-Turban" assignment and her faithfulness in wearing each one her students came up with, including the Viking helmet and Alien headdress.

And of course we all remember the elation of that April day in 1993 when we cheered Maria on as she finished in the top 200 in the senior women's division of the Oldtown Marathon. It seemed for a brief, happy time that her recovery was complete.

But even when the cancer recurred and Maria had to undergo painful and debilitating therapy, she always made time to see colleagues and former students, encouraging them to talk freely about her disease and to ask questions.

Maria's originality, dedication, compassion, and courage will be deeply missed.

Maria's family has established the Maria Gomez Performing Arts Fund to support bringing outside performers to Dewey School and taking classes on field trips to local plays and concerts. If you wish to make a donation, you may send it to the school office.

Clara Kowalski
Principal

4

Press Releases and Press Kits

How do you publicize an event, service, or product? The classic public relations method is to create your own news story about it and circulate the story to newspapers and radio and television stations as a press release.

4a Press Releases

A press release is a clear, readable account of information you want to get into the public eye. Like a news article, it should begin with a strong lead and use the inverted pyramid order (see pp. 29–30). Press releases can be general or targeted. A general release like Sample 27 (p. 70) is typically sent to larger newspapers or television stations and gives an overview of the story. A targeted release like Sample 28 (p. 73) focuses on specific areas of interest to cable news stations, local papers, alumni and professional newsletters, or radio stations. As its name implies, a targeted release is tailored to the narrower needs of the publication it is aimed at.

Press releases usually follow the format of a classic news story, with subtle variations depending on what paper or station you are targeting. A surprising number of press releases are printed unchanged in newspapers or read as news stories on the air. Papers and stations often have small staffs, so they welcome well-written releases.

To get your releases published you need to anticipate the needs of the paper's editor, the person who will be your first reader. Connect your release to key issues the paper covers; learn the editor's pet peeves about press releases. Be especially careful about inflated, hyped-up copy, which goes over well with some editors but will destroy your credibility with others.

MIDTOWNE MEDICAL CENTER
111 MAIN STREET
MIDTOWNE, TX 70001

FOR IMMEDIATE RELEASE

Contact: Alberta Foote
Public Relations
(222) 525-5555

MIDTOWNE MEDICAL CENTER ELECTS OFFICERS

The medical staff of Midtowne Medical Center elected new officers at its annual meeting on March 10: Dr. Henry Galen, president; Dr. Marian Merck, vice president; and Dr. Alfred Chang, secretary-treasurer. Each will serve a two-year term.

Completing their terms of office were Dr. Anna Green, president; Dr. Henry Galen, vice president; and Dr. Ludwig Patel, secretary-treasurer.

Dr. Galen joined the Midtowne Medical staff in 1979. An internist and urologist, he is chief of the hospital's Urology Center and served as secretary-treasurer of Midtowne Medical prior to his vice presidency.

Dr. Merck specializes in oral and maxillofacial surgery and has been on the Midtowne Medical staff since 1966. She has been chair of the Ambulatory Care Committee and medical director of the hospital's Ambulatory Care Unit since its creation in 1983.

Dr. Chang, a urologist who joined the Midtowne Medical staff in 1976, chaired the hospital's Infection Control Committee from 1985 to 1989.

Midtowne Medical Center is a 489-bed regional hospital that provides a full range of medical and surgical services, with special expertise in cardiology, gynecology, oncology, oral and maxillofacial surgery, and urology.

—30—

Press Release Format

HEADING The heading, which appears at the top of the first page, includes:

- the logo or letterhead of the organization (here, Midtowne Medical's letterhead)
- the release time (here it's "FOR IMMEDIATE RELEASE," or it could state the date: "FOR RELEASE OCTOBER 3, 1996")
- the name and phone number of the person to contact for more information. (The contact name may also go at the end.)

TITLE Like a headline, the title highlights the most newsworthy aspect of the release. (See pp. 30–32 for more on what makes a story newsworthy.) The title is located prominently and typed in uppercase letters, boldface type, or both.

LEAD As in journalistic practice, this lead covers most of the Five W's and an H—*who*, *what*, *where*, *when*, *why*, and *how*—leaving out only the *why*.

BODY The body follows inverted pyramid order, starting with the most interesting or pertinent information and ending with the most routine or peripheral. (See pp. 29–30 for more detail about inverted pyramid order.) Generic information about the organization comes at the end or even in an attachment (see p. 78).

LAYOUT The layout follows the general guidelines on margins for business letters ($1\frac{1}{2}$ inches all around) as well as some of the conventions derived from newspaper practice.

- The body is double spaced to give the editor room for changes.
- The last page (even if the release is only one page long) ends with a dash, the numeral 30, and a dash (—30—) to indicate that there is no more copy. If the release is longer than one page, all pages but the last end with a dash, the word *more*, and another dash (—more—). A longer release would also place a shortened heading, or *slug*, giving its topic, followed by the page number, at the top right corner of each page after the first (for example, "Midtowne Medical Officers   2").

Writing Press Releases

Whether you work for a community organization, a nonprofit group, or a large corporation, you may need to "get the word out" through press releases. Since your success depends on placing stories in the local media, you need to know a few basics of public relations writing.

AUDIENCE AND STYLE Who is the audience for your press release? This depends on where you are sending it. A large newspaper or television station with a wide audience is more likely to assign your story to a reporter than to print or broadcast your release itself. In this case, your main audience is the editor or news director, and your job is to highlight the information you think will convince him or her to cover the story. Think of yourself as providing raw material rather than a finished product. Keep the release short—a single page if possible—and factual; provide more detailed information in attachments or in a full press kit (see pp. 78–79).

On the other hand, many small newspapers and newsletters will print a well-written release as is. In such a case your main audience is the reading public, and you act as the reporter, deciding on the angle, style, and selection of details.

What style should you adopt for your release? How creative can you be? The best answer is to read past releases issued by your organization as well as articles on similar topics in the publications on your mailing list. Keep a clippings file and compare what appears in print with what you write. In time, you'll learn how to convey the right image for your organization while tailoring your releases to specific topics, to the styles of particular publications, and to the interests of certain editors. The more your release reads like a real story, the better its chance of getting printed as is.

For example, Sample 28, written like a news story, uses a formal, neutral style suitable to its content and the dignity of the organization sending it. It would likely appear in the business section of a large metropolitan newspaper, where it would be read by medical or business professionals. Samples 29 and 31, more like feature stories, use question leads, direct address, informal style, and colorful, enthusiastic language to promote entertaining events sponsored by organizations less concerned with maintaining a dignified image. These would probably be printed unchanged by small local newspapers.

This version of Sample 27, sent to the local paper, offers detailed personal and professional information about the new president.

MIDTOWNE MEDICAL CENTER
111 MAIN STREET
MIDTOWNE TX, 70001

FOR IMMEDIATE RELEASE   Contact: Alberta Foote
Public Relations
(222) 525-5555

Gives name and number of contact person

SMALLTOWN RESIDENT ELECTED
TO MEDICAL CENTER STAFF

Highlights Smalltown connection

Dr. Henry Galen of Smalltown will serve as president of the medical staff at Midtowne Medical Center for the next two years. An internist and gastroenterologist, Dr. Galen lives on Maple Street with his wife Velma and their two children, Keith, 8, and Alice, 5.

Focuses on Galen, the local resident, with additional personal information

Dr. Galen received a fellowship from the Wellness Clinic Foundation, interned and took his residency at Midstate University Hospital, and graduated in 1977 from North Central Medical College, where he was a member of the Omega Omega medical honor society. He moved to Smalltown in 1979 when he joined the staff at Midtowne Medical Center.

Adds detail about this local resident

Also elected at the March 10 meeting of the Midtowne Medical staff were Midtowne resident Dr. Marian Merck, vice president, and Dr. Alfred Chang of Heartland, secretary-treasurer. Each will serve a two-year term.

Gives information about other officers, of less local interest, later in release

Midtowne Medical Center is a 489-bed regional hospital providing a full range of medical and surgical services, with special expertise in gynecology, oncology, oral and maxillofacial surgery, and urology.

Places generic information about organization at end, so editor can cut

—30—

A lively, informal style is appropriate for this release about a parade at the local mall. Written by a public relations agency, this release aims to get free publicity for the client, knowing that an article about a family parade is likely to be welcome in local papers. Attached might be a schedule of events, a brochure on the mall, and captioned photos of the band.

**VILLAGE GREEN MERCHANTS ASSOCIATION
35 STATE HIGHWAY
OLDTOWN, MA 01211**

FOR IMMEDIATE RELEASE

Includes names of two local businesses as well as catchy description of event

VILLAGE GREEN, OLDTOWN TRUST TO SPONSOR
MARDI GRAS PARADE FEBRUARY 18

Uses direct address as appropriate to light-hearted subject

Oldtown, MA—Superman and the Power Rangers, ghosts and witches, Michael Jackson and Madonna—you can find them all at the second annual Village Green/Oldtown Trust Mardi Gras Parade at the Village Green Mall on Sunday, February 18.

Mentions familiar landmarks along parade route

Open to costumed marchers of all ages, the parade begins at the mall's south entrance at 1:00 P.M. Stepping to the Dixieland sounds of Oldtown's own Back Street Ramblers, marchers will wind through the lower level to the Vil-

Gives names and job titles of emcees to satisfy client

lage Landing Food Court, where Mayor Jane Olansky and Stan Miller of WOBR radio will emcee the award ceremonies.

As marchers pass the reviewing stand, members of the Village Green Merchants Association and local dignitaries will pick the two best-costumed adults to be King and Queen of the Mardi Gras. The winning costumes in three junior age categories will become carnival princes and princesses.

Shows there is more on next page

—more—

74

Led by the newly crowned royalty, the parade will continue through the mall's upper level, ending at the Ice Cream Emporium, where all participants will receive free cones and gift certificates redeemable at participating Village Green stores.

Marchers should gather in front of the Oldtown Trust branch on the lower mall no later than 12:45 P.M. The band will strike up the march at 1:00 P.M. sharp.

Details how to join near end, so nonmarchers can skip this part.

Cosponsors of the event are the Village Green Merchants Association and the Oldtown Trust Company. The Village Green Merchants Association is dedicated to making the Village Green a center of community activities. The VGMA sponsors an annual Thanksgiving food drive and free December holiday concerts, and donates uniforms and equipment to Oldtown's youth sports programs.

Includes generic promotional paragraph (also called "boilerplate") at end; will include or cut depending on available space

—30—

For further information, contact: Malcolm E. Winter
Winter Public Relations
111 Elm Street
Oldtown, MA 01211
(225) 355-3345

Names contact person at end instead of beginning; either place is OK

This informational release is formal and neutral in style. Its primary purpose is to reach people who can benefit from the program. Since the organization has money to award, it assumes that it needs only to get the news out rather than aggressively recruit applicants.

**OLDTOWN COMMUNITY
DEVELOPMENT CORPORATION
300 ELM STREET
OLDTOWN, MA 01211**

States specific release date so Oldtown CDC does not get inquiries before this date

FOR RELEASE MARCH 1, 1996
Contact: Al Carter (508) 545-5225

HOME REPAIR GRANTS AVAILABLE TO SENIORS

Oldtown seniors unable to afford repairs to their homes may soon find help from a new program funded by the Wright Foundation and available through the Oldtown Community Development Corporation.

Appeals to potential fund recipients

Under the Senior Home Repair Program, income-eligible Oldtown residents 62 and older may apply for grants of up to $5,000 to cover the cost of essential home repairs such as leaking roofs, broken windows, rotted or damaged stairs, or faulty plumbing. Not covered under the program are cosmetic renovations such as painting, tiling, and floor refinishing.

Gives information about funding agency to help donor get positive publicity

Funding the program is the Wright Foundation, a private nonprofit group based in Chicago and dedicated to addressing the needs of low- and moderate-income senior citizens. The total amount of the foundation's grant to the Oldtown CDC is $150,000.

Provides dates and how to apply at end

Applications will be available beginning March 10 and must be submitted by April 1. Oldtown CDC Director Al Carter expects grants to be awarded around May 1. For application forms and information on eligibility, seniors can call Al Carter at 545-5225.

—30—

SAMPLE 31: HUMOROUS PRESS RELEASE

The headline attempts to catch the eye, first, of the local editor and, then, of the public. The style may increase the chances that the editor will print it as is, though a staid paper might balk at the hype that pervades this piece. Attachments could include a full schedule of activities, a brochure or fact sheet on the fund drive, and captioned photos of last year's fair.

ACADEMY SCHOOL PTA
P.O. BOX 23
TOWN HIGHLANDS, NH 11911

FOR IMMEDIATE RELEASE   Contact: Ida Prentis
PTA President
(603) 474-4144

DUNK YOUR DAD FOR FATHER'S DAY AT THE

ACADEMY SCHOOL FUN FAIR JUNE 15

Stumped for the perfect Father's Day gift? Treat your dad to a dip in the dunk tank at the Academy School's annual Fun Fair on Saturday, June 15, from noon to 4:00 p.m. at the school playground on Academy Road.

> Grabs reader with question lead and plays up Father's Day angle

All dads accompanied by a kid 16 or under are automatically entered in a drawing for a getaway weekend for four at the Surfside Inn in Seabreeze. But the catch is that the winning dad has to take a seat over the dunk tank and give each of his kids three chances to hit the target that triggers the dunk.

> Delays information on how dad gets dunked to the second paragraph, keeping readers' interest

The Fun Fair offers plenty for the rest of the family too. Preschoolers will enjoy the hourly puppet shows by Margie's Magical Mummers; older kids can play games of chance, ride a camel, or make Dad a gift at one of the many craft activity tables; and everyone can browse at the used book sale or pick up some vegetable or flower flats to fill in those bare spots in the garden.

> Uses colorful, informal style to enliven an otherwise flat listing of day's events

All proceeds from the fair benefit the Academy School Library Fund. Rain date is Sunday, June 16.

—30—

ACCURACY You are responsible for the accuracy of all information in your releases. Be sure that names are spelled correctly, that job titles and descriptions are accurate, that dates and every checkable detail are correct. You'll feel foolish if you misspell the name of the new company vice president or get the time of a lecture wrong so that a speaker addresses a virtually empty room. Inaccurate publicity can be worse than no publicity at all.

Attachments and Press Kits

ATTACHMENTS To keep a release brief and lively, offer detailed supplementary information in attachments rather than in the body of the release. Such attachments might include:

- backgrounders (in-depth explorations of associated contexts or issues)
- fact sheets to back up claims in the release
- informational brochures on your company or organization
- relevant policy statements issued by your organization
- biographies of persons prominently mentioned in the release
- timetables of activities for an event the release promotes
- a calendar of upcoming events sponsored by your organization
- appropriate photographs (with identifying captions)
- lists of photographic or video opportunities
- copies of relevant articles or recent press coverage of your group's activities

For example, Sample 28, on Midtowne Medical Center (p. 73), could be accompanied by detailed biographies of each of the officers, a captioned photograph of the incoming and outgoing officers, and a general informational brochure on the medical center.

PRESS KITS Sometimes, especially if your organization calls a press conference or holds an event to announce a new product or kick off a fund-raising campaign, you may want to distribute a press kit to media representatives either ahead of time or at the door. The simplest press kit consists of a press release and a selection of attachments, usually organized in a two-pocket folder.

In organizing a press kit, you should:

- place the two most important materials—usually the press release and a factsheet, backgrounder, or timetable—at the front of the pocket on each side of the folder.
- place the rest of the materials behind these, the more important ones closer to the front.
- attach a cover letter on letterhead paper to the front of the folder. This letter should state the main purpose of the press conference or event and should prominently list the contents of the press kit.

Photos and Photo Captions

Sometimes a picture is worth a thousand words—or at least the hundred or two you might expend on a short press release. For example, a local paper in Coldtown, Maine, might decide to run the following item (which amounts to free publicity for several businesses) only because a picture of a local person enjoying a break in sunny Mexico would be appealing to snowbound readers in mid-February. The caption identifies *who* is in the picture, naming the organization or group they represent, *what* they are doing, and *where* they were when the photo was taken.

SAMPLE 32: PHOTO CAPTION

Bonnie Hamilton (first row, second from left) of Coldtown Travel and other area travel agents prepare to depart for Cancun, Mexico. Metropolitan Travel of Boston sponsored the recent trip to familiarize travel agencies with the Cancun area's lagoons, ruins, and hotels. Guests were flown by Delta Airlines and spent four days at the newly remodeled Hacienda Hotel—Cancun.

5
Flyers and Brochures

Do you need to advertise a product or service? Do you want to announce a workshop, lecture, performance, conference, or job opening? recruit volunteers? make people aware of an issue or problem? If so, a flyer or brochure can reach the people you want. But which should you choose?

If your message is simple and you want to reach a lot of readers at a low cost, a flyer is your best bet. Handing out flyers on a busy street or posting them in strategic locations can reach a lot of people cheaply. On the other hand, if what you need to promote or advertise is more complex, or if attracting users or patrons depends on the specifics of what you offer (a list of every session at a conference, the precise ingredients in the pest control chemicals used by a lawn and garden service), you probably need a brochure. Though a brochure costs more, it provides more space for details, allows for an attractive design, and is likely to be kept for future reference.

You also need to consider how you will produce the brochure or flyer. Turning out a finished-looking product used to mean giving your material to a print shop, which would take charge of design, layout, and typography. Today, widely available software programs and laser printers make it possible to turn out professional looking flyers and brochures on your own; all you pay for is paper and the means of reproduction.

This chapter offers basic principles of copywriting and design for the most common types of flyers and brochures. Whether you are producing your own or working with a printer, this chapter will help you decide what to say, how to say it, and how to use the layout to make your message stand out.

Which Health-Care Option Is Right for You?

Learn about important changes in health-care coverage
from AWU negotiator Sheila Brown.

Health-Care Information Forum
sponsored by
Allied Workers' Union

Wednesday, November 5
3:30 to 5 p.m.
Corcoran Center

Hear speakers from five plans, including two new HMOs:

- Alpha Beta Health Plan
- Amalgamated Mutual Benefits Plan
- Bayside HMO
- Central City Community Health Plan
- Healthworks HMO

Talk with representatives from each plan.
Learn what you need to know.

**Enrollment Period for New Health-Care Plans Ends
November 30.**

Make the Right Choice!

5a Flyers

Flyers are one-page advertisements or announcements—mini-posters meant for bulletin boards or hand distribution. You may fold them in half or in thirds to mail them, but their text does not fall into separate panels corresponding to the folds, as it would on a brochure. Though flyers come in all shapes and sizes, this chapter focuses on the most common format: a single $8\frac{1}{2} \times 11$ inch sheet, printed on one side only, with text and visuals oriented to what professionals call the "portrait" format in which the vertical dimension is the longer one. (The other choice is "landscape," where the 11-inch side is the horizontal.)

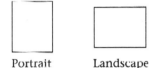

Portrait   Landscape

Flyer Format

Sample 33 would be suitable both for posting and for handing out to Allied workers.

VISUALS The graphic of doctor and patient visually conveys the health-care theme. Printing this flyer on colored paper will make it stand out on a crowded bulletin board or wall and will help workers locate it among other notices they receive.

HEAD In bold, large type (on a full-size flyer, this would mean one-half to one inch tall), the head speaks clearly to a current issue of major concern to Allied workers. The question head makes the issue personal and immediate in a way that a head like "New Health-Care Options" would not.

SUBHEADS Boldface and color highlight the most important points. Date, time, and place get lines of their own.

TEXT The chunked and bulleted text communicates information quickly and easily; a busy worker can get the picture in less than a minute. The imperative verbs "learn," "hear," and "talk" address readers directly and call for their active response. Bulleting the list of five options dramatizes the fact that there are more choices now.

FOOT A final, bold, large-type statement reminds readers of the urgency of the issue and visually balances the composition.

Planning a Flyer

AUDIENCE AND STYLE Who do you want your flyer to reach? Are you writing to employees or group members who need only abbreviated references to organizations, titles, and locations, or to outsiders who need everything spelled out? To insiders already committed to a cause or to potential clients who need to be roped in by a catchy head? Step one is to imagine your audience and design a strategy and style suited to them. Style in a flyer involves not only tone and wording but also the overall visual effect, including graphics and color. The catchy phrasing, hand lettering, pastel paper, and cartoon drawings perfect for a flyer for a pre-school playgroup would be all wrong for announcing upcoming student government elections or advertising a resume service.

VISUAL DISTANCE Headings need to be visible from a walk-by distance of 5 to 10 feet, and text needs to be readable at the arm's-length distance people usually keep from a bulletin board or wall full of notices. (Some, like help-wanted signs in store windows, may need a headline legible from a passing car.) To attract and hold the attention of walk-by readers long enough to get your message across, observe these guidelines:

- Set the head in type at least half an inch tall and get readers' attention in a way appropriate to the content—a clear, straightforward heading for announcing a conference or meeting ("Handicap Access Legislation Update"), an appeal to goodwill in calling for volunteers ("Help Us Help the Homeless"), a witty twist in marketing a service ("Is Your Pup Turning into a Couch Potato? Let Deb's Dogwalking Service Help").

- Attract attention to the main theme of the flyer through layout and design. Colorful paper, borders, and thematically appropriate graphics can catch readers' eyes and make them stop for a look. But make sure the design is appropriate to both the organization and the topic. A spare, high-tech look with a modern typeface and a bold border may be just the thing for an up-and-coming design consultant or a help-wanted ad for a software retailer but too slick and impersonal for recruiting soup-kitchen volunteers or host families for foreign-exchange students. Make the flyer reflect your group's level of sophistication and formality.

NOTE: *Beware of graphics that work against your message. A flyer on a college campus had an eye-catching graphic of a stylized tree branch laden with blossoms. Not being in search of gardening (or possibly decorating) advice, most students avoided taking a closer look and were surprised to discover it was a notice for a spring series of computer workshops. The designer chose the wrong motif to emphasize: the graphic should have drawn attention to computers, not the season.*

- Text should be brief, laid out to emphasize key points, and easy to digest in the five to ten seconds readers usually spend scanning posted items or handouts thrust upon them. Clear subheads, short sentences, lively verbs, and easy-to-grasp lists invite people to pause and read rather than move on.

ESSENTIAL INFORMATION It is surprisingly easy to forget something essential in putting together your flyer. So here is a checklist based on the five W's of journalism. Make sure you include:

- *WHAT* What is happening, what is offered, or what you are asking of readers.

- *WHO* Who is appearing, sponsoring an event, offering a service, or asking for help. If readers aren't likely to recognize the names of speakers, sponsors, or service providers, add identifying tags—Dana Getty, licensed day-care provider; Bill Jordan, decorated Vietnam veteran; Gloria Gomez, director of Affirmative Action for Allied Insurance; Good Shepherd House, a provider of care for the terminally ill since 1987.

- *WHERE* The location of an event (including address and directions if the flyer is for people outside the organization); where to call or write for service or information; the location of an organization soliciting volunteers (the name of a town or small city may be enough, but in a large city you may wish to specify the area or neighborhood).

- *WHEN* The day(s) and date(s) of a meeting, lecture, performance, or conference ("Thursday, April 4" is clearer than the date alone or than "Thurs. 4/4"); the hours and days of the week when services are available, when readers can call for information, or when volunteers may work.

- *WHY* Persuasive evidence of why readers should attend an event, make use of a service, volunteer their time, and so forth. This *why* should be evident throughout the flyer. In

Flyers

Sample 33, for example, the foot most explicitly indicates why workers should attend the session, but the reason is also implicit in the heading ("Learn") as well as in the bulleted list of five options, including the two new ones.

CREATIVE IMITATION Each time you walk past a bulletin board, notice which flyers attract your attention and figure out why. Keep notes on flyers that you think are suitable in design and approach for your intended audience. Analyze what makes them work well and adapt some of their approaches to your next flyer.

SAMPLE 34: FLYER ADVERTISING A SERVICE

Gets readers' attention

Dramatizes problem in amusing graphic

Clarifies problem consultants propose to solve

Displays name prominently in context of offering help

States qualifications and gives overview of services

Highlights strong points in bulleted list

Gives professional affiliations to authenticate qualifications

Lists phone and fax numbers to tell how to contact firm

Feeling Crowded Out of Your House?

No place to put things— but no money for expensive additions?

Let CREATIVE SPACEMAKERS help.

As experienced professional interior-design consultants, we can help you make better use of your existing closet and storage space. We can also recommend low-cost improvements to add new storage areas without disrupting your living space.

We offer:

- Free initial consultations in your home
- Evening and weekend hours
- Affordable prices
- Local references

Lucy Arabedian, ASID
Sonia Goldberg, ASID

Phone: (707) 535-5555
Fax: (707) 535-1110

Three Hours of Your Time Can Feed over 200 Hungry People

When you volunteer at the
Oldtown Food Depot

WHAT YOU CAN DO

- Spend a morning or afternoon volunteering at the Oldtown Food Depot.
- Help sort and pack donated food from local supermarkets for distribution to local soup kitchens and after-school programs.
- Meet other friendly people who care about the hungry in our community.

WHO WE ARE

A nonprofit organization with a small paid staff, the Oldtown Food Depot relies mainly on volunteer labor to sort and pack the donated food it receives each week. We train crews of 30–40 volunteers per 3-hour session to work in assembly-line fashion to process the food quickly and reliably. While a few jobs require heavy lifting, others simply involve inspecting food containers.

HOW TO VOLUNTEER

Volunteer individually for 3-hour morning or afternoon sessions Monday through Friday, or get together a group of eight or more from your business or organization and join one of our two Saturday sessions.

To sign up for a date and time, call Volunteer Coordinator Dan Edwards at (707) 222-2522 weekdays between 10 A.M. and 4 P.M.

OLDTOWN FOOD DEPOT
300 Commercial Way
South Oldtown, MA 01002

Uses direct address to dramatize how little time can produce big results

Identifies organization

Organizes text in chunks with headings

Continues conversational mode of head

Sets foot in large type to balance head and identify organization from walk-by distance

Names position clearly

Highlights company name, gives overview of services, and describes ideal candidate

Highlights qualifications and experience needed and points to attractive features of job

Uses simple border for professional look

Balances head visually and states how to apply for job

Clarifies hiring policies

Marketing Coordinator

The Human Services Jobmart, a bimonthly publication filled with job listings, news, and information for the Delmarva human services community, seeks a creative go-getter to develop and coordinate its marketing efforts.

The Human Services Jobmart needs someone with:
- initiative
- excellent writing skills
- experience working with human-services providers
- ability to work as a team player

The Human Services Jobmart offers:
- congenial, stimulating work environment
- opportunities for rapid advancement
- generous benefits package
- competitive salary based on qualifications

If you meet these requirements and wish to grow with a fast-moving new company, we want to hear from you. Send resume to:

Human Services Jobmart
372 Tidewater Drive
Bayshore, MD 30002
Attention: Laura Ward

An Equal Opportunity Employer

5b Brochures

If flyers are miniposters, brochures are more like minibooks. And unlike flyers, brochures are folded so they can easily be mailed or put in a pocket. The text and design elements in brochures are organized in panels that correspond to the sections made by the folds.

Brochures can range from simple, inexpensive, single-color text on white or colored paper to eye-catching, full-color productions with photos and graphics on textured or glossy stock. To choose the right style of brochure, consider your company or group image, the readers you are addressing, and your budget. Think first about the message different quality brochures will send. If you're advertising a luxury resort or pricey custom-made shirts with a low-budget brochure, or if you promise "rock-bottom prices" on house painting in an oversized glossy, full-color brochure, your medium will undermine the credibility of your message.

You should also become familiar with the great variety of professional materials and programs available for producing a brochure, including paper stock with paneled graphics and spaces where you may insert text, and computer software programs that provide graphics and format your text for you. See "Resources" (pp. 201–3, 211) for one of the best of these. But you still need to know some basics of brochure design and strategy so that you, rather than your software, are in control of this improtant piece of promotional material.

While brochures come in a number of sizes and folding patterns, this chapter focuses on the most common: the $8\frac{1}{2} \times 11$ inch sheet folded into three panels, with the fold on the left and the opening on the right, as with a book.

Typical letterfold brochure, opening from the right, like a book

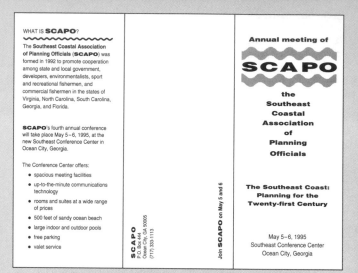

WHAT IS **SCAPO**?

The Southeast Coastal Association of Planning Officials (**SCAPO**) was formed in 1992 to promote cooperation among state and local government, developers, environmentalists, sport and recreational fishermen, and commercial fishermen in the states of Virginia, North Carolina, South Carolina, Georgia, and Florida.

SCAPO's fourth annual conference will take place May 5–6, 1995, at the new Southeast Conference Center in Ocean City, Georgia.

The Conference Center offers:

- spacious meeting facilities
- up-to-the-minute communications technology
- rooms and suites at a wide range of prices
- 500 feet of sandy ocean beach
- large indoor and outdoor pools
- free parking
- valet service

SCAPO
P.O. Box 444
Ocean City, GA 50005
(717) 333-1113

Join **SCAPO** on May 5 and 6

Annual meeting of

SCAPO

**the
Southeast
Coastal
Association
of
Planning
Officials**

**The Southeast Coast:
Planning for the
Twenty-first Century**

May 5–6, 1995
Southeast Conference Center
Ocean City, Georgia

Panels A, B, and C of brochure
(outside panels, with cover panel at right and address panel in middle)

Planning for the Twenty-first Century

FRIDAY EVENING SESSION

Welcome: Max Winston, SCAPO Chair

Panel Discussion

Tourism, Economic Development, and the Environment: An Overview

Sandra Alberg, Alberg Enterprises

Barry Jones, South Carolina Office of Coastal Zone Management

Olivia DiGregorio, Seaside City Planning Director

Dana Schwartz, Virginia Economic Development Commission

SATURDAY MORNING SESSION

Panel Discussions

Recreational Uses and Coastal Ecosystems

Walter Talltrees, Save Our Shores

Abner Mahlon, Southeast Association of Sport Fishermen

Andrea Finkelstein, Department of Marine Biology, Tidewater University

Steven Beaumont, South Carolina Department of Tourism

OR

Single-Family Development: The Hidden Costs

Jordan Atkins, Edgewater County Zoning Commission

Melanie Zimmer, Department of Urban Planning, Sunbelt University

Hubie Whiteside, Metropolitan Development Corporation

Atha Poulakis, Affordable Housing Initiative

SATURDAY AFTERNOON SESSIONS

Workshops

Environmental Regulation Update

Leader: Carol Neslow, EPA

Preparing the Environmental Impact Statement

Leader: Jonathan Wong, Wong and Bell Associates

Innovative Zoning in Coastal Tourist Areas

Leader: Luella Gaskins, Alton County Zoning Board

Using the Design Review Process to Preserve Community Character

Leader: Calvin Walden, Seaside City Planning Department

SATURDAY EVENING SESSION

Video Presentation and Discussion

Sunrise Township: A Model for Partnerships between Developers, Environmentalists, and Local Government

Leader: Max Winston, Outer Banks Association

REGISTRATION FORM

Registration deadline: May 14

I plan to attend the following sessions:

_____ Friday, May 5, 5 to 10 p.m. (includes dinner) $80

_____ Saturday, May 6 , 9 a.m. to 5 p.m. (includes continental breakfast and full lunch) $100

_____ Saturday, May 6, 5 to 10 p.m. (includes dinner) $80

_____ Amount Enclosed or Charged

I am paying by

_____ check (make payable to **SCAPO**)

_____ Mastercard _____ VISA

Acct # _____

Exp. Date _____

Cardholder name _____

Signature _____

Name: _____

Address: _____

City: _____

State: _____ Zip: _____

Phone, with area code: _____

Mail to:

SCAPO
P.O. Box 444
Ocean City GA 50005

Fax credit card payment only to:
(717) 333-1111

Panels D, E, and F of brochure
(inside panels)

90

Brochure Self-Mailer Format

This self-mailer brochure neatly packages the announcement of the conference, some details about its sessions, a mailing panel, and a registration form.

OUTSIDE PANELS Panel A, the outside left panel, contains interesting but inessential information since it is on the back of a registration or order form that may be detached and returned. If you put your organization's address and phone number here, be sure that this is not the only place where they appear.

Panel B, the outside center panel, is the mailer panel, allowing the brochure to be mailed without an envelope. SCAPO's phone number is included beneath the return address on this panel, so that readers will have that information even after the registration form has been detached and returned.

Panel C, the outside right panel, is the cover—the panel readers will see first. So this is the place to make your pitch well enough and attractively enough that readers want to open the brochure and read what's inside. Since SCAPO may want to leave piles of brochures out on tables, the cover's main head is large enough to be read by people scanning from a distance of three to four feet. The conference title is in the top third of the panel, so it will be visible if the brochure is placed in a display rack.

INSIDE PANELS Panels D and E, the inside left and center panels, interact, though a different brochure might treat them as separate columns. Here, the conference schedule continues from the left to the center panel, and the head that spans both panels visually alerts readers to the connection between them.

Panel F, the inside right panel, is the registration form to be completed and returned. On a different kind of brochure, you could replace this registration form with a contribution or order form. Alternatively, you could put the return form on the outside left panel. This would allow you to use all three inside columns for related text and visuals, though you would have to be careful not to put essential information on the back of the registration form.

Panel A when brochure is unfolded, with cover panel at right

Panel A when brochure is folded

WHAT IS **SCAPO**?

The **Southeast Coastal Association of Planning Officials** (**SCAPO**) was formed in 1992 to promote cooperation among state and local government, developers, environmentalists, sport and recreational fishermen, and commercial fishermen in the states of Virginia, North Carolina, South Carolina, Georgia, and Florida.

SCAPO's fourth annual conference will take place May 5–6, 1995, at the new Southeast Conference Center in Ocean City, Georgia.

The Conference Center offers:

- spacious meeting facilities
- up-to-the-minute communications technology
- rooms and suites at a wide range of prices
- 500 feet of sandy ocean beach
- large indoor and outdoor pools
- free parking
- valet service

[Panel B]

SCAPO
P.O. Box 444
Ocean City, GA 5G005
(717) 333-1113

Join **SCAPO** on May 5 and 6

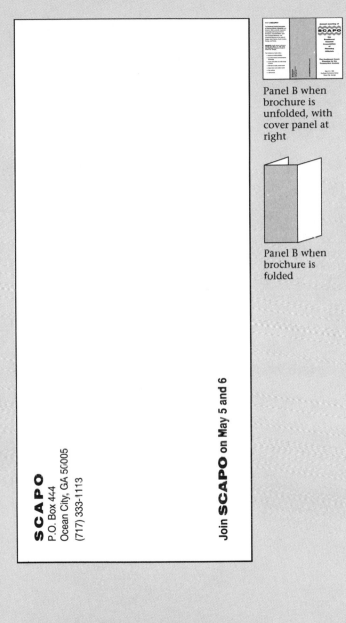

Panel B when
brochure is
unfolded, with
cover panel at
right

Panel B when
brochure is
folded

93

Panel C when
brochure is
unfolded, with
cover panel at
right

Panel C
(cover panel)
when brochure is
folded

Annual meeting of

the
Southeast
Coastal
Association
of
Planning
Officials

The Southeast Coast:
Planning for the
Twenty-first Century

May 5–6, 1995
Southeast Conference Center
Ocean City, Georgia

Planning for the Twe

FRIDAY EVENING SESSION

Welcome: Max Winston, SCAPO Chair

Panel Discussion

Tourism, Economic Development, and the Environment: An Overview

Sandra Alberg, Alberg Enterprises

Barry Jones, South Carolina Office of Coastal Zone Management

Olivia DiGregorio, Seaside City Planning Director

Dana Schwartz, Virginia Economic Development Commission

SATURDAY MORNING SESSION

Panel Discussions

Recreational Uses and Coastal Ecosystems

Walter Talltrees, Save Our Shores
Abner Mahlon, Southeast Association of Sport Fishermen
Andrea Finkelstein, Department of Marine Biology, Tidewater University
Steven Beaumont, South Carolina Department of Tourism

OR

Single-Family Development: The Hidden Costs

Jordan Atkins, Edgewater County Zoning Commission
Melanie Zimmer, Department of Urban Planning, Sunbelt University
Hubie Whiteside, Metropolitan Development Corporation

Atha Poulakis, Affordable Housing Initiative

Panel D when brochure is unfolded (inside of brochure)

Panel D when brochure is folded

95

[Panel E]

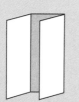

Panel E when brochure is unfolded (inside of brochure)

Panel E when brochure is folded

nty-first Century

SATURDAY AFTERNOON SESSIONS

Workshops

Federal Environmental Regulation Update

Leader: Carol Neslow, EPA

Preparing the Environmental Impact Statement

Leader: Jonathan Wong, Wong and Bell Associates

Innovative Zoning in Coastal Tourist Areas

Leader: Luella Gaskins, Alton County Zoning Board

Using the Design Review Process to Preserve Community Character

Leader: Calvin Walden, Seaside City Planning Department

SATURDAY EVENING SESSION

Video Presentation and Discussion

Sunrise Township: A Model for Partnerships between Developers, Environmentalists, and Local Government

Leader: Max Winston, Outer Banks Association

REGISTRATION FORM

Registration deadline: May 14

I plan to attend the following sessions:

_____ Friday, May 5, 5 to 10 p.m. (includes dinner) $80

_____ Saturday, May 6, 9 a.m. to 5 p.m. (includes continental breakfast and full lunch) $100

_____ Saturday, May 6, 5 to 10 p.m. (includes dinner) $80

_____ Amount Enclosed or Charged

I am paying by

_____ check (make payable to **SCAPO**)

_____ Mastercard   _____ VISA

    Acct # _____

    Exp. Date _____

    Cardholder name _____

    Signature _____

Name: _____

Address: _____

City: _____

State: _____ Zip: _____

Phone, with area code: _____

Mail to:

    SCAPO

    P.O. Box 444

    Ocean City GA 50005

Fax credit card payment only to:

    (717) 333-1111

Panel F when brochure is unfolded (inside of brochure)

Panel F when brochure is folded

Designing a Brochure

Brochure format depends on several factors: paper size, number of folds, the folding pattern, and whether the brochure goes in an envelope or is a self-mailer. We illustrate two of the most common brochure styles: the three-panel self-mailer, and the three-panel non-mailer, both folded letter style, as in Samples 37 and 38.

PANEL PLAN In planning the panels of your brochure, visualize how they will work when the brochure is folded. For example, in the drawings on p. 99 and in Samples 37 and 38, you can see how the three panels look on the flat sheet before it is folded. The outside is especially tricky, since the cover panel will actually be at the right-hand side of the sheet.

Most commonly, text follows the panel divisions and is arranged in short, readable chunks. Headings, graphics, and visuals (such as photographs) can either be contained within a single panel or can cross over panel divisions, prompting the reader to see a continuity between the columns of text. For example, in Sample 37, the heading unites the left and center panels, which contain the conference program.

LAYOUT Presenting text in chunks, separated by white space, makes for a more readable brochure. Variation in type size and the use of bullets, boxes, and illustrations or graphics make the text more readable and more pleasing to the eye. For professional books on these aspects of layout and design, see "Resources" (pp. 206–7).

The figures below show a few common patterns for layout of the inside of a three-panel brochure. The top portion of the drawing shows a staggered pattern for text and illustrations or graphics, the middle shows a diagonal pattern, and the bottom shows how an all-text brochure can use headings, boxes, and centering to produce a diagonal pattern of organization.

COVER When you walk by a table full of brochures, which ones do you pick up first? If you're looking for a summer camp for your child, do you reach for the one that says "Camp Shawmut" or the one that advertises "A Magical Summer" with a photo of smiling children in a canoe on a wooded lake? If you're seeking investment advice, do you pick up the one inviting you to "Get a Piece of the Money Action" or the one promising "Personalized Professional Investment Counsel-

Common layout patterns for
inside of three-panel brochure

ing"? The cover of a brochure can be serious or humorous, can inform or provoke curiosity; you need to choose an approach that fits your organization or service and the users or supporters you hope to attract.

Most brochures for workshops, conferences, causes, or services take the standard approach of giving readers a capsule of the who, what, where, and when. Sample 37 uses a header to identify the sponsoring organization (who), a title and subhead to name the theme of the conference (what), and a footer to give the date and location of the conference (when and where). A brochure for a nail salon might have a cover with the head "Manicures: Which Style Is Right for You?" (what), with the salon name (who) as a subhead, and the address (where) and hours of operation (when) at the bottom.

Other brochures may use their covers to provoke interest or curiosity. The heads "Common Myths about AIDS" or "Do You Know Where Your Cat Is?" invite readers to open the brochure and find out their misconceptions about AIDS or learn that their cats need to be immunized against rabies.

BROCHURE TEXT Clarity and brevity are the hallmarks of a successful brochure. Brochures give a brief picture of the conference, service, or cause they are promoting. Those interested in finding out more can ask for supporting literature such as the full conference program, consumer pamphlets or booklets, position statements, or annual reports.

REPLY OR ORDER FORM—A SPECIAL CAUTION When readers detach and return a reply or order form, they lose whatever is on the back. So keep essential information on panels that will not be detached and returned. It's a common oversight for novice brochure makers to list the name, address, and phone number of the sponsoring organization only on the panel that backs the order or reply form. This leaves readers with no place to turn if they want to make changes or get more information.

What OCSC Does for the Oldtown Community

Here's what your neighbors say:

"When my husband left me and I had to go back to work, OCSC saved my life by offering affordable **preschool daycare** for my toddler and three-year-old."

"My father was depressed and lonely after Mom died, but the **Senior Lunch and Social** gave him something to look forward to and a way to make new friends."

"My wife's alcoholism was ruining our family, and we didn't know where to turn. OCSC gave us the **family counseling** and **support groups** we needed, and helped us get my wife into a substance abuse program."

"We know lots of parents whose kids go out drinking every weekend night. OCSC's **Teen Drop-In Center**, with its Friday night social activities, gives our son and his friends a place to go and be 'cool' without getting into trouble."

Board of Directors

Donna S. Gelrich
Vice President, Bank of Oldtown
Rev. Emmanuel Iantosca
Pastor, Saint Elizabeth's Church
Clara Kowalski
Principal, Dewey Elementary School
Martin R. Lechner
President, Lechner Associates
Keesha Wagner
Director, Oldtown Elder Services Commission

OCSC Staff

Beulah Johnson, Director
M.S. in Social Services, Oldtown University
Karen Albertson, Preschool Daycare
B.A. in Early Childhood Education, Caritas College
Arnold Shavel, Counseling Services
M.S.W., University of the Southwest
George Williams, Afterschool and Teen Activities
B.A. in Education, Upstate University
Helen O'Malley, Senior Services
M.S. in Gerontology, Caritas College
Michael Buchanan, Summer Camps
B.S. in Physical Education, Academia College

OLDTOWN COMMUNITY SERVICE CENTER

Serving the Oldtown Community for over 80 years

**777 Walnut Street
Oldtown, MA 01002
(617) 888-8228**

Panels A, B, and C of brochure
(outside panels with cover at right and address panel in middle)

What the Oldtown Community Services Center is

Founded in 1914, the Oldtown Community Services Center is a private, nonprofit organization offering free or low-cost programs and services to families, seniors, and teens in the metropolitan Oldtown area.

What OCSC offers

Preschool Daycare
Help for working parents five days a week through a licensed daycare program for children ages 1 to 5.

Afterschool Programs
Physical activities, arts and crafts, and supervised homework programs weekday afternoons for children in grades K–6.

Senior Lunch and Social
A free nutritious lunch, card and board games, and a chance to get together with friends Monday through Saturday, 11 A.M.–2 P.M.

Teen Drop-In Center
Free or low-cost supervised athletic and social activities for teens in grades 7–12 Tuesdays and Thursdays, 3–6 P.M. and Fridays, 8–11 P.M.

Family Counseling and Referral Program
Help with family issues, substance abuse, and eldercare decisions; free initial consultation and sliding-scale fees.

Summer Day Camp
For boys and girls ages 7–12; supervised by OCSC staff on beautiful Clearwater Lake in the Westwoods Nature Preserve.

Join OCSC and Help Us Keep Serving Oldtown Families, Seniors, and Teens.

Please enroll me as a:

____**Supporting Member: $100**
Supporting members receive discounts on preschool, afterschool, and summer camp tuition.

____**Contributing Member: $50**

____**Friend: $10 or more**

All contributors to OCSC receive our quarterly newsletter and notification of special events.

Contributions are tax-deductible. Make checks payable to OCSC.

Name_____

Address_____

City_____State____Zip_____

Please send me brochures on the following OCSC programs:

____Family Counseling and Referral Service

____Preschool and Afterschool Programs

____Summer Camp

Panels D, E, and F of brochure
(inside panels)

[Panel A]

Panel A when brochure is unfolded, with cover panel at right

Panel A when brochure is folded

Uses testimonial quotes interesting enough for right-hand panel when readers first unfold cover, but that contain no essential information to be lost when contributor/order form on back is returned

Highlights names of programs in testimonial quotes

What OCSC Does for the Oldtown Community

Here's what your neighbors say:

"When my husband left me and I had to go back to work, OCSC saved my life by offering affordable **preschool daycare** for my toddler and three-year-old."

"My father was depressed and lonely after Mom died, but the **Senior Lunch and Social** gave him something to look forward to and a way to make new friends."

"My wife's alcoholism was ruining our family, and we didn't know where to turn. OCSC gave us the **family counseling** and **support groups** we needed, and helped us get my wife into a substance abuse program."

"We know lots of parents whose kids go out drinking every weekend night. OCSC's **Teen Drop-In Center,** with its Friday night social activities, gives our son and his friends a place to go and be 'cool' without getting into trouble."

102

Panel B when brochure is unfolded, with cover panel at right

Panel B when brochure is folded

Shows staff is qualified by listing credentials

Board of Directors

Donna S. Gelrich
Vice President, Bank of Oldtown
Rev. Emmanuel Iantosca
Pastor, Saint Elizabeth's Church
Clara Kowalski
Principal, Dewey Elementary School
Martin R. Lechner
President, Lechner Associates
Keesha Wagner
Director, Oldtown Elder Services
Commission

OCSC Staff

Beulah Johnson, Director
M.S. in Social Services, Oldtown
University
Karen Albertson, Preschool Daycare
B.A. in Early Childhood Education,
Caritas College
Arnold Shavel, Counseling Services
M.S.W., University of the Southwest
George Williams, Afterschool and
Teen Activities
B.A. in Education, Upstate University
Helen O'Malley, Senior Services
M.S. in Gerontology, Caritas College
Michael Buchanan, Summer Camps
B.S. in Physical Education, Academia
College

Panel C when
brochure is
unfolded, with
cover panel at
right

Panel C
(cover panel)
when brochure is
folded

Uses type that makes
name of organization
easy to read from
three to four feet
away

Does not specifically
make fund-raising
pitch

Gives address and
phone number on
cover, a panel not to
be detached

OLDTOWN
COMMUNITY
SERVICE CENTER

*Serving the Oldtown Community
for over 80 years*

777 Walnut Street
Oldtown, MA 01002
(617) 888-8228

What the Oldtown Community Services Center is

Founded in 1914, the Oldtown Community Services Center is a private, nonprofit organization offering free or low-cost programs and services to families, seniors, and teens in the metropolitan Oldtown area.

What OCSC offers

Preschool Daycare
Help for working parents five days a week through a licensed daycare program for children ages 1 to 5.

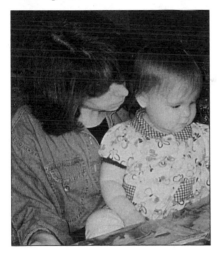

Afterschool Programs
Physical activities, arts and crafts, and supervised homework programs weekday afternoons for children in grades K through 6.

Panel D when brochure is unfolded (inside of brochure)

Panel D when brochure is folded

Shows OCSC's history and status as a nonprofit

Does not specifically make fund-raising pitch

Uses boldface type to highlight OCSC's programs and services

Places photograph at top of lower half of panel to balance photo in next panel

Panel E when
brochure is
unfolded (inside
of brochure)

Panel E when
brochure is
folded

Gives times and days
for senior and teen
programs, since
these have no
separate brochure

Omits information on
hours, fees (separate
brochures available),
but specifies ages,
sexes, so parents
know if camp is
suitable

Senior Lunch and Social
A free nutritious lunch, card and board
games, and a chance to get together with
friends Monday through Saturday, 11 A.M.–
2 P.M.

Teen Drop-In Center
Free or low-cost supervised athletic and social activities for teens in grades 7–12, on
Tuesdays and Thursdays, 3–6 P.M., and Fridays, 8–11 P.M.

Family Counseling and Referral Program
Help with family issues, substance abuse,
and eldercare decisions; free initial consultation and sliding-scale fees.

Summer Day Camp
For boys and girls ages 7–12; supervised by
OCSC staff on beautiful Clearwater Lake in
the Westwoods Nature Preserve.

Join OCSC and Help Us Keep Serving Oldtown Families, Seniors, and Kids.

Please enroll me as a:

____ **Supporting Member: $100**

Supporting members receive discounts on preschool, afterschool, and summer camp tuition.

____ **Contributing Member: $50**

____ **Friend: $10 or more**

All contributors to OCSC receive our quarterly newsletter and notification of special events.

Contributions are tax-deductible. Make checks payable to OCSC.

Name _____

Address_____ _____

City_____State__ __Zip__ ____

Please send me brochures on the following OCSC programs:

____Family Counseling and Referral Service

____Preschool and Afterschool Programs

____Summer Camp

Panel F when brochure is unfolded (inside of brochure)

Panel F when brochure is folded

Emphasizes OCSC's service to community

States benefits of making a large contribution

States clearly how to make out check

Leaves spaces for requesting other brochures, allowing this to double as order form

6
Reports and Proposals

The business of the world gets done through reports and proposals. These are action documents, prepared to accomplish precise goals and usually written to order. The managers or supervisors who ask for reports or proposals have specific purposes in mind: to keep themselves informed; to make decisions about personnel, practices, or operations; to decide whether or not to fund particular projects.

6a Reports

A report can be two paragraphs in a letter detailing a recent inspection visit or two thousand pages investigating problems at a nuclear power plant. Most reports cover routine matters:

- progress on a small construction project
- the best site for a new bank branch
- a monthly update on sales
- a comparison of two brands of printers
- the Student Senate's year-end review

But some reports can have a national impact, such as the reports on the Challenger disaster or the assassination of President Kennedy.

This chapter concentrates on the most common report strategies and formats. It pays special attention to the context of the report, since reports succeed when they meet the needs of their readers—the people who request them—and fail when they don't. Knowing what your readers want is the first step toward becoming a successful report writer.

QUINTANA DISTRIBUTORS
SLOANSVILLE FRUIT DIVISION
222 WEST 11TH STREET
CHICAGO, IL 61111

| TO: | Victor Quigley, Manager | DATE: | March 4, 1996 |
| FROM: | Kathleen Armstrong, Quality Control | SUBJECT: | Progress report on freezer units |

PROBLEM AND RECOMMENDATIONS:

On February 26 I was asked to check on the freezer units in the Division Street warehouse. Three complaints of spoilage had occurred in the preceding six months.

After a careful inspection, I can report that the units are performing within specifications. However, two new latches (total cost: $700) will make the freezers perform better and eliminate complaints. I recommend we install the latches.

INVESTIGATION:

On February 28 I visited the Division Street warehouse and inspected the freezers with Mr. Aldo Vukovitch, Chicago representative of Freeze King, the manufacturer of the compressor units. A two-hour examination of all six freezers indicated that they were operating properly, though minor maintenance was needed on one freezer. Based on the tour, Mr. Vukovitch and I ruled out a manufacturing defect.

On March 5 I interviewed Aaron Mellon, warehouse manager, who said the three problems with spoilage could be traced to unit 4, on the south side of the building.

Three warehouse workers I interviewed on March 5 told me that the doors of freezer units 4 and 6 were often hard to close. Sometimes they had to exert extra force on the units to engage the catch. If the doors don't latch properly, the temperature cannot be maintained. Mellon and the warehouse workers believe that new latches are needed.

SOLUTION:

I recommend that we replace the latches on freezer units 4 and 6. A local vendor, Tuft Stop, Inc., quoted a price of $349.95 per latch, installed. If you authorize it, I can have the latches installed by Friday. A follow-up inspection will determine whether the new latches solve the problem.

Report Format

Sample 39 shows one of four formats for a report (memo, letter, chapter, or book); choice of format depends on the report's complexity and the organization's style. Here Armstrong's one-page memo was enough to cover a single problem.

PROBLEM (INTRODUCTORY SUMMARY) The problem or issue, food spoilage, is stated briefly, followed immediately by her recommendations. In a short report like this, problem and recommendation may be combined in a paragraph or two. In a longer report a one- or two-page summary may follow the recommendation.

INVESTIGATION (THE BODY) Armstrong organizes her report chronologically, noting the date she was asked to investigate the problem and the dates she made her visits. She names significant people, but omits her account of calling Freeze King to make an appointment with Mr. Vukovitch, since that isn't important.

SOLUTION (RECOMMENDATION OR CALL FOR ACTION) This appears twice, once as part of the opening summary and once in greater detail at the end. In this case, the recommendation is a request for the manager's authorization to spend $700. Since this report is about an investigation Armstrong was asked to undertake, her recommendations are perfectly in keeping with her task.

Writing the Report

Since writing an effective report depends on knowing what the reader wants, many organizations prescribe a format or require a printed form to organize every step. This is particularly true for routine matters, such as a real-estate firm's sales reports, a hospital's medical reports, or an investigation team's accident reports. Undoubtedly, these strict formats limit a writer's freedom, but in return they provide the security of a fixed outline.

In many important cases, however, there will be no form to follow. Then it will be up to you to decide exactly what should go into a report. Sometimes the manager will want information; other times the manager will expect recommendations, since you will be closest to the situation and therefore in a good position to supply them. Here the manager requesting the report on the freezer units had a problem: spoiled food in the warehouse. He detailed Kathleen Armstrong from Quality Control to investigate the problem, track down the cause, and make a recommendation. Her report connects to the initial request, describes the problem, and gives her recommendation, all in a single paragraph. This follows the key principle of giving the most important information first. Quigley can read Armstrong's first paragraph and know what's in the entire report. For further details he can read her account of how she got her information (names of company informants and of a local vendor). Armstrong meets Quigley's needs for information and offers a recommendation backed by expertise.

How will you know what your report should include? Well-run organizations will often provide the writer of a major report with written specifications, usually in the form of a memo stating the report's purpose, scope, expected completion date, and, if necessary, the budget and personnel available to help. If you're not given such a list, it's up to you to ask questions about what's expected when the report is assigned. You should also look at similar reports. This is all part of the report-writing process—finding out what is expected before you write.

The length of your report and the format you choose (memo, letter, chapter, or book) depends on the report's complexity and the organization's style. Sometimes a simple memo or letter will be sufficient (as in Sample 39, p. 110). Other times you'll need a more formal memo, a chapter length (10–50 page), stapled or informally bound report, or even a book with chapters. The more complex the report, the more it needs navigation tools like a table of contents, section headings and subheadings, and appendices.

No matter what form the report takes, certain features remain the same. Reports should present information in the order the reader needs it, not in the order the writer learned it. The current situation and the action recommended should come first, background and history later.

OPENING SUMMARY OF PROBLEM OR ISSUE Since reports are almost always requested by someone in authority who wants to be kept up to date (progress reports or routine monthly sales and activity reports) or who needs to make a decision (feasibility studies or informational reports), the most important information should come up front. The problem or issue should be stated briefly, followed immediately by recommendations (if appropriate).

The principle behind this format is the same as for newspaper leads: busy readers—managers and executives in the case of reports—want issues, plans, and recommendations clearly presented. They don't want to wade through a lengthy document to discover the point, the solution, or the costs.

BODY The body of the report should:

- detail the problem
- state the objective
- explain the methodology
- summarize the results
- point to the key issues
- justify the recommendations.

The body of the report is the place for detail and full explanations. Like Sample 39, many reports tell about an investigation in chronological order. Others compare and contrast or detail specifications.

RECOMMENDATION OR CALL FOR ACTION If recommendations are appropriate for your report, they should appear twice, once quite briefly in the opening summary and once in detail in a final, concluding section. But not every report needs recommendations. If you were asked to provide background or to research some figures or personnel, then recommendations might be superfluous or inappropriate. The important thing to keep in mind is that a successful report fulfills the requirements of the reader and does so clearly and concisely.

The Language of Reports

A report should reflect the writer's position in the organization, not his or her personality. This means that individual flourishes, highly personalized vocabulary, and idiosyncratic stylistic quirks are out. Unfortunately, far too often report writers, fearful of sounding too personal, take refuge in the dull and drab "official" style that quickly causes the brain to fog over.

LEVELS OF FORMALITY How can you sound human without sounding too personal? Study reports you like and that seem to work in your organization. Look for the level of formality successful report writers have used. Does your organization encourage using "I" and "we," as Armstrong's progress report for Quintana Distributors does? Or does it insist on the seemingly objective, impersonal style? Here are the ranges to look for:

Dull impersonal style	It was discovered by means of interviews conducted by an investigator that . . .
Good personal style	In my interviews I found that . . .
Good impersonal style	Interviews revealed that . . .

Note that the dull version uses passive verbs ("was discovered," "conducted"), while the better versions use active verbs, verbs that show the subject doing something ("I found," "Interviews revealed"). Passive verbs make for passive readers; use them only when you want the report to sound official and detached. (For more on passive verbs, see pp. 185–86.)

TONE You need to determine what tone someone in your position should take in making recommendations. The following three sentences all make essentially the same point, but they all take different stances:

Strong, forceful	The only way Consolidated can compete is by closing the Belmont plant.
Moderate	Closing the Belmont plant seems a good way for Consolidated to remain competitive.
Tentative	In order to remain competitive, Consolidated might explore the feasibility of closing the Belmont plant.

How do you want to sound? Are you in a position of some authority, writing to peers or subordinates? Then a strong, forceful presentation may work best. Are you a fairly new junior person writing for a committee of higher-ups? Then forcefulness may seem presumptuous, while a more tentative tone will convey both your willingness to consider all possibilities and your recognition that the decision-making authority is not yours. Choice of tone should depend on your readers' preferences, your relationship to them, and your organization's traditions. Confer with experienced writers over matters of tone, and look at the tone of previous successful reports.

6b Proposals

Proposals make things happen. They tell a person or agency what you'll do, when you'll do it, and how much it will cost. A telecommunications company sends an $18,000,000 proposal offering to handle all telephone service for the New York State Department of Motor Vehicles. A scientist submits a research proposal for $90,000 to a drug company. An administrative assistant proposes that she be given a week's release from her customary duties to rearrange the secretarial pool. In all three cases the written proposal is the action document. Based on that proposal, readers will decide whether to answer yes or no. This section will examine four different kinds of proposals.

SOLICITED Solicited proposals are usually submitted in response to a written announcement or request for proposals (RFP) that states specific guidelines. Since such proposals are judged in an open competition, with readers rating them on how well they meet the guidelines, you must follow the terms and structure of the RFP. Deadlines are especially important; late proposals are non-starters.

UNSOLICITED Unsolicited proposals, usually to sell a service or product to an organization that has not announced its desire for such a service or product, are tougher. Instead, you'll have to come up with your own way to demonstrate that there is a problem or need, and then you'll have to offer a solution. The solution counts most, but unless the proposal establishes a need, readers won't invest resources.

INTERNAL A proposal from within an organization can often be more informal than those submitted from outside. Nevertheless, you'll still need to have a good plan; in fact, if you are part of the organization, a poor proposal can hurt your reputation. In internal proposals you'll usually know some of the readers, but your writing should proceed under the assumption that unknown people will be part of the decision-making process. Choose the tone, the terms, and the examples that will make the proposal appropriate for all possible readers, not just for the ones you know.

EXTERNAL A proposal from outside an organization is usually more formal, since the readership is part of another company, a funding agency, or a branch of government. The classic proposals most people are familiar with are solicited grant proposals to funding agencies and solicited business proposals for providing goods or services.

We will also look at how proposals are judged, since knowing what readers want helps writers to submit successful proposals.

The writer proposes to set up new procedures to cut down on customer complaints.

BEMIS BANKCORP
111 EAST 12TH STREET
DUNSTER, IOWA 12233

To: Ann Curley, Manager   Date: April 4, 1996
From: Tamara Bailey,   Subject: Line control in
Customer Service   branches

OVERVIEW:

I request a two-week reassignment to institute more effective line control at four of our busiest branches. At the end of the period I will submit a report on the effectiveness of the new methods.

PROBLEM:

Customers at our four busiest branches—Waterloo, Davenport Central, Dunham, and Bussey—have complained about the length of the teller lines, especially at midday. The complaints have risen significantly, since we had a 25 percent reduction in tellers in April. To keep our customers from going to another bank we need a cost-effective way of moving teller lines along quickly. I propose to institute a new system at four busy branches, test its effectiveness, and report back to you within two weeks. If my plan is successful, Bemis will be able to handle increased crowds without hiring new tellers.

PLAN

I want to introduce a next-available-teller queue in the four branches. Currently we have a line in front of each available teller's window. This can result in excessive waiting, especially when one customer has a complex transaction. The proposed system will avoid excessive waits at individual windows and move crowds along faster.

PERSONNEL:

One person, myself, for two weeks, full time. I am familiar with teller queues from my years spent at Harris Bank in Chicago, where we introduced them in 1990. My customary duties will be assumed by Jim Nardone and Althea Hargreaves, who know my job and have filled in for me when I have been on vacation.

COSTS:

No financial outlays. We have lightweight stands, inexpensive rope, and some signs.

TIME FRAME:

May 1–14; report to be submitted May 14.

Proposal Format

OVERVIEW The opening section of this internal, unsolicited proposal provides a short, easily digestible summary of what the proposal is about, who the key players are, and how much time it will take. Although Bailey addresses someone she has discussed the idea with (her manager) her report is complete enough for any reader to understand it.

PROBLEM This section details the problem or need the proposal addresses. In Bailey's case the problem is customer complaints over long lines. She doesn't go into great detail, since her manager knows about the problem. In the world of banking customer complaints and long lines are commonly understood to be serious problems that need attention.

PLAN Bailey's plan spells out the solution in detail. She simply wants to apply a common solution to the bank branches. She uses the phrase "next-available-teller queue" because everyone in her business knows that phrase quite well.

PERSONNEL Bailey includes this section even though the task she's proposing is a one-person job. She describes her familiarity with the procedures she wants to institute to show her qualifications for the task.

COSTS This is often the decisive category. For this project the costs are practically zero. But most proposals have a more substantial budget, and in many cases the budget would be examined separately by qualified accountants. (See Sample 41, p. 120, for a budget example.)

TIME FRAME She specifics how long the work will take and when it will start. This short, simple task will be accomplished in two weeks, so Bailey pins down beginning and ending dates.

EVALUATION This is a common category in proposals. Some proposals, like Bailey's, do not include an evaluation section, but promise a later evaluative report. Some managers want to fine tune evaluation by pointing to specific figures. Note, however, that Bailey does include specific expectations—reducing waiting time and eliminating consumer complaints—that allow her experiment to be evaluated.

Writing a Proposal

A proposal is an argument, full of assertions, claims, and promises. It says you'll do something to satisfy the reader and that you're the best person or organization to do the job.

Proposals compete in two ways. First and foremost, they compete with other, quite valid claims on the organization's or agency's resources. So your proposal needs to justify spending precious resources on your particular project. This is especially important with unsolicited (or "blind") proposals. Second, when your proposal responds to an RFP, you must show that your proposal is better than the competition.

PROPOSALS IN CONTEXT Before writing the proposal, learn all you can about the needs and outlook of the company or funding source. Your proposal has to show how your idea or plan will fit in with the aims of the people with the money. How do you find out their aims? The RFP, if there is one, and company material such as annual reports, can give you an idea of the organization's priorities and philosophy.

If the proposal has been solicited, you can also ask for help from agency or company personnel designated to answer questions. Some common questions: Has anything like this been tried recently? Are you currently sponsoring (or purchasing) X? How long a proposal are you looking for? How will it be judged? Little of this is secret or proprietary information; your competitors are likely to know the answers, and you should too. In many cases, agency or company staff will comment on early drafts or go over guidelines with you. They will often be particularly helpful with first-time proposal writers. Tell them, "We are moving into this field for the first time" or "We've never sent your group a proposal before." Don't be surprised at the open reception you get; it's in the company's or funding agency's interest to get as many good proposals as possible.

On the other hand, you can't count on help from your proposed client for an unsolicited proposal. Keep in mind that an unsolicited proposal runs the risk of seeming like a "cold call," a telephone call out of the blue to an uninterested customer. But since you probably won't want to spend time working out a detailed proposal unless you have some idea that it may succeed, you can try to lay the groundwork through conversations, discussions, and an understanding of the organization's ways of doing business before tipping your hand about what you propose.

How Proposals Are Judged

People who make decisions about solicited proposals are usually working from a checklist, often a set of questions requiring yes or no answers or responses scaled 1 to 5. (Low-level staff will have eliminated any proposals that didn't meet the deadline or were missing key parts.) An assessment form like the one following is commonly used by one federal agency that solicits large numbers of proposals in the field of education.

State in one to three sentences what this proposal sets out to do.

On a 1 to 5 scale, with 1 as lowest and 5 as highest, rate this proposal:

1. How well does the proposal respond to the RFP? ☐

2. Does the problem or need seem significant? ☐

3. Do proposers have an appropriate plan? ☐

4. Do proposers have appropriate personnel? ☐

5. Do proposers have an appropriate budget? ☐

These questions do not allow reviewers much leeway, and they certainly do not allow for unsupported global judgments. The numerical rankings allow easy comparison of different proposals, with a perfect score in all 5 areas giving a maximum of 25 points. Knowing how the proposals in such competitions are ranked, experienced grant writers take special pains to spell out precisely how their proposals respond to the RFP. Less experienced writers who assume that readers will understand this can get low scores on item 1. Experienced writers also know that only 5 points out of 25 (20 percent of the total score) go for the quality of the plan, which after all is the actual idea behind the proposal. These writers worry less about an innovative or exciting plan than a high-quality overall proposal, knowing that high ratings in every single category are needed to win. Of course nothing beats a good idea, but in this type of competition ideas in themselves are not enough. The proposal stands

A small consulting firm responds to an RFP for a survey of internships.

LOPEZ ASSOCIATES
RESEARCH, WRITING, AND EDITING

PROPOSAL FOR RESEARCH ON INTERNSHIP OPPORTUNITIES

SUMMARY

Focuses on Albuquerque, home of U. of New Mexico, as required by RFP

The New Mexico Division of Employment (NMDE) has requested a comprehensive survey to determine what college-level internships exist in the Albuquerque area. Lopez Associates proposes to produce a report describing the number and type of internships offered to college students by a carefully selected cross section of Albuquerque businesses and governmental agencies. Lopez Associates, an experienced professional research firm that has conducted many surveys, will complete the report in four weeks. Cost: $3,180.

NEED

Picks up major question directly from RFP

NMDE statistics report that fewer than 10 percent of New Mexico college undergraduates take internships, and fewer than 5 percent of New Mexico employers regularly sponsor interns. Are additional New Mexico businesses and governmental agencies willing to sponsor internships? Lopez Associates will answer that question in a report detailing the internship opportunities in Albuquerque. With the results of this report, NMDE can publicize internship opportunities, and the University of New Mexico can enlarge internship programs.

PLAN

Uses NMDE statistics, since proposal is going to same agency

Conduct a telephone survey of a cross section of at least 100 Albuquerque employers drawn from the following sectors (percentages based on NMDE statistics representing job share):

Employer	Percent
federal government	20
state government	15
city and county government	10
manufacturing	20
service	20
sales	15

Using this survey, the report will show:
1. specific internship opportunities, listed by sector.
2. willingness of employers to train students.
3. awareness of internships among employers.

PERSONNEL

Rosita Lopez (resume enclosed), president of Lopez Associates, holds an M.A. in professional communications from Rensselaer Polytechnic Institute and a B.A. in management from Fort Lewis College, Durango, Colorado. She worked as an analyst for the California Division of Personnel and served as project manager for the U.S. Department of Commerce in Albuquerque. She has ten years' experience as an independent consultant, working in business, education, and research.

TIMELINE

The project will take four weeks.

Week one	Telephone survey (35 companies and agencies)	Details projected number of calls per week
Week two	Telephone survey (35 companies and agencies)	
	Progress report	
Week three	Telephone survey (30 companies and agencies)	
Week four	Compilation of report in draft form	
	Final report	

BUDGET

All work to be done at Lopez Associates' standard rate of $20 per hour.

Personnel		
Planning for survey: 5 hours	$100	Allows agency to see how money will be allocated
Telephone survey: 120 hours	2,400	
Progress report: 5 hours	100	
Final report: 20 hours	400	
Telephone	120	
Supplies, copying	60	
Total	$3,180	

or falls on its overall quality, not on one or two of its high points.

Of course, not all competitions are decided this way, and another kind of competition might produce a very different proposal. Some organizations and agencies welcome strong, innovative ideas and will work with you to flesh them out into solid proposals. In that kind of situation, the quality of the idea matters more than anything else, so the proposal stands or falls on the conception itself, not its implementation.

NOTE: *In many cases, readers will make a general judgment about the budget, but professionals will also examine it separately. Especially complex proposals (to renovate a power plant, to design a new airliner) that may well involve hundreds or thousands of pages require separate groups of experts to read and evaluate the budget, the technical design, and the management plan.*

7

Instructions and a Few Points about Manuals

Sooner or later, someone may ask you to write a set of instructions or procedures. If you're good at it, you may even get to do a whole manual. But where do you begin?

7a Instructions

Instructions range from highly specialized directions for technical experts to explanations aimed at a general audience. For example, you may be asked to write assembly or operating directions for purchasers of a company product, safety or security procedures for new employees, or highly technical instructions for your programmers on the use of new software.

Instructions and manuals have certain characteristics:

- direct address to an identifiable set of readers with specific needs
- the expectation of some action or result from those readers
- the need for precision, clarity, and conciseness
- the use of layout and sometimes graphics to augment the text

This chapter gives the principles for writing instructions aimed at novice users and technical instructions aimed at experts. At the end, it offers some special advice about manuals.

HOW TO SOLDER AN ELECTRONIC CONNECTION USING THE SPEE-DEE 110 SOLDERING IRON

OVERVIEW

The Spee-dee 110 soldering iron lets you make neat and secure electronic connections.

SUPPLIES

- Your Spee-dee 110 soldering iron
- Spool of 60/40 grade rosin core (NOT acid core) solder
- Wire cutter/stripper
- 4/0 (0000) grade steel wool or 280 grade or finer sandpaper
- small-nosed pliers

PREPARATION

1. Support your Spee-dee soldering iron on its prop with the tip at least 1 inch away from any surface. Turn the control knob to the low-heat setting. The iron is ready when the light comes on.
2. Using the wire cutter/stripper, cut the wire(s) to the desired length, and strip the insulation from about $\frac{5}{8}$ inch of the end(s).
3. Make sure the stripped metal ends of the wires are clean and bright. If they are not, clean them with the steel wool or sandpaper. The solder will adhere well to them only if they are clean.
4. Twist the stripped metal ends of the wires together with your fingers or the pliers.

SOLDERING THE CONNECTION

5. Using the pliers to hold the wires, heat the metal ends of the wires by holding the soldering iron on them. DO NOT HEAT THE SOLDER ITSELF. The hot wires will melt the solder.
6. Still holding the wires with the pliers, draw the solder slowly along the heated ends. The solder will melt in a second or two and flow into the joint.
7. Taking care not to move the joint, IMMEDIATELY slide the hot solder off the joint. Do not wait until the solder cools slightly or the connection will be rough.
8. Continue to hold the joint still for 10 to 20 seconds or until the solder cools and sets. Blow on the joint to speed cooling.

EVALUATION

Once the joint is fully cooled, examine it visually. The joint should be shiny and fully covered with the solder. If it is greyish or has visible gaps, use the Spee-dee 110 to unsolder the joint and try again. Heat the joint with the gun, and separate the components carefully, grasping the wires by their insulated sections. It is not necessary to remove all the old solder, but be sure to add some new solder when you redo the joint.

Format for Instructions

These instructions for a tool manufactured by the writer's company are aimed at novices, but the writer makes certain assumptions about what those readers know or can best find out elsewhere. If they are using the soldering iron to secure electronic connections, presumably they have some expertise or at least other sources of information on how to design the project and assemble its parts. The writer also assumes that readers know how to use a wire cutter/stripper. These are instructions for the use of the tool only, not a do-it-yourself book on home electronics.

OVERVIEW The opening section gives the user an overall grasp of the task to be done.

SUPPLIES The writer lists all the parts, tools, and materials so that users won't have to stop in the middle to search for things they didn't know they'd need. Here, the bulleted format makes the five items easy to see. Where the type or grade of materials makes a difference, the descriptions are precise—60/40 grade solder, 4/0 steel wool, etc.

INSTRUCTIONS Instructions are organized into groups with headings, so that the number of steps in each section is fairly small.

- The steps are numbered sequentially across sections so users hastily scanning the instructions as they juggle equipment can't mistake Step 2 in the first section for Step 2 in the second.
- The writer addresses readers directly throughout, using "you" and clear imperative verbs like "plug in," "cut," and "twist."
- Steps are listed in the order in which users need them. Since the soldering iron needs time to heat up, turning it on is listed as the first step, even though the iron will not actually be used until Step 5. Each step is clear and brief.
- Directions are as specific as possible; for example, users are not told to keep the soldering iron tip "a safe distance away from any surface," since they may not know what that safe distance is, but are instructed to keep it "at least 1 inch away."
- The "Evaluation" section advises users on how to make sure they've done the job right—and what to do if they haven't.

Writing Instructions

Well-written instructions are crucial to the satisfaction of customers and the efficient performance of employees. Yet all too often instructions are not well written. A survey of students in an advanced professional writing class revealed some common problems they had with instructions or manuals for equipment they owned:

- The language was too technical; unfamiliar terms were not defined.
- It was hard to find out how to do specific things because there was no index or the index was poor.
- Steps were left out.
- Instructions assumed knowledge readers lacked.

Interestingly, the students generally rated their technical aptitude as average to above average, but reported that their actual proficiency on equipment they owned was only basic to average. Given such complaints, the gap may well be due to the poor quality of the instructions for that equipment.

Two situations can arise in organizations: you are asked to write instructions because you know how to do a procedure, even though you're not an experienced writer, or you are asked to write instructions because you're an experienced writer, even though you know little or nothing about the procedure and have never written a manual. Both situations have their pitfalls. If you are an expert on the procedure, you may find it difficult to imagine what novice users need to know; if you are an experienced writer but not an expert on the procedure, you may identify with novice users so fully that you won't even know what questions to ask. The answer in both situations is to pick the brains of others to supply what is missing.

The technical expert needs to find out from novice users what they need to know before they start, what terms they don't understand, at what points they become confused. The best way to do this is to observe novices trying to use drafts of the instructions. Some software companies have special rooms with one-way glass through which instruction writers can do exactly this.

On the other hand, the writer who lacks the technical expertise needs to start with questions and periodically consult the technical experts to make sure that his or her understanding is correct and that the instructions will produce the desired results. This writer can use his or her own learning process as a guide to determine the needs of novice users.

KNOWING YOUR READERS The first step in writing instructions is figuring out who your readers/users will be. You can't determine what information you need to include or where to start unless you know what your readers do and do not know. In writing instructions on using a new software package, are you addressing novice users or programmers already familiar with existing company systems? Sometimes, the answer will be both, so you'll need to figure out how to address novice users' needs in a section experts can skip over. But many times, you'll be able to pinpoint a narrower group of readers and write for them.

CHOOSING THE RIGHT STYLE When writing instructions, you'll need to pay special attention to the following guidelines:

- Keep sentences short. Users of instructions need to get information quickly and in small, manageable chunks.
- Use positive language. Say "wear a protective helmet," not "don't leave your head unprotected."
- Keep terms consistent. Whenever you refer to the same object or process, refer to it by the same term. Using the same word over and over is not bad style—it's consistency.
- Make the tone conversational and address the reader directly. Say "turn on the power" rather than "the power must be turned on."

WRITING USER-FRIENDLY INSTRUCTIONS

- Organize instructions from the standpoint of the user's needs, building the sections of your instructions around common scenarios for using the procedure or item. For example, a good VCR manual might focus major sections on how to play prerecorded tapes and how to record programs from television. While this point seems pretty obvious, an amazing number of manuals and instructions are organized instead from the standpoint of how the system is designed. For example, the instructions for many computer modems are organized key by key. This means that the novice user can find out how to change the baud setting only by looking through the list of keys to discover which one covers "setup" or "installation" or "configuration."

- Ask yourself whether readers will use your instructions as a linear guide (e.g., to set up a machine), as a reference to find answers to specific questions, or as both.
  - Organize linear sections by beginning with the very first thing the user needs to know and proceeding step-by-step to the very last thing. Don't leave anything out or take anything for granted; experienced users will skip the easy stuff,

SAMPLE 43: TECHNICAL INSTRUCTIONS

These instructions for a camcorder power adapter assume users know where to connect the power cord to the camcorder—or at least know or can observe that each type of connection on a piece of video equipment is configured differently so that they can match up the type of connecter and number of pins in it to the corresponding jack on the camcorder.

HOW TO USE THE AJAX AB-111 AC POWER ADAPTER

Gives an overview of what the adapter does

The AB-111 AC power adapter allows you to operate any camcorder on regular household current for an unlimited time without having to change or recharge batteries.

Warns users of a potential negative effect

CAUTION: To avoid battery damage **turn the power switches on both devices to "off"** before connecting the AB-111 power adapter to the camcorder.

Omits parts list, since needs are obvious

Begins steps with simple, direct-address verb

Distinguishes between name of switch (all caps) and name of setting (in quotes)

1. Set POWER SELECT switch on the AB-111 power adapter to "CAMERA."
2. Connect one end of the DC power cord to the camcorder.
3. Connect the other end of the DC power cord to the AB-111 adapter.
4. Set the POWER SELECT switch on the camcorder to "12 V DC INPUT."
5. Turn on the POWER switch of the camcorder.
6. Turn on the POWER switch of the AB-111 power adapter.

Alerts users to possible hazard just before point when it could occur

NOTE: *Always turn off the POWER switch on the AB-111 power adapter when you turn off the power on the camcorder. Leaving the adapter on while the camera is turned off can cause the camcorder battery to discharge.*

but novices will need it. One of the most common failings of instructions on how to program your VCR is not telling novice users that the VCR clock must first be set to the correct time (including A.M. or P.M.) and day of the week.

- Organize reference sections such as glossaries alphabetically or in some other way that is obvious and convenient for readers. A clear table of contents or an index allows many sets of instructions or manuals to double as reference tools.

- Refer users to an appendix or to other sections of the instructions for information that some users are likely to need, but that would be distracting to cover at this point.

- Group the steps in the process in logical categories under easily understandable headings, so that users can see which stage of the process they are working on.

FOLLOW UP The final section of a set of instructions may indicate ways to evaluate the success of the actions users have taken, may discuss potential problems and tell how to avoid or correct them, may note exceptions or special cases, may offer a troubleshooting list, or may suggest further applications once the user becomes more expert.

WARNINGS Always state such warnings in the instructions BEFORE the danger or problem may occur. Cautions applying to the entire process can go in a separate section at the beginning. Cautions applying to particular steps should come just before those steps. In either case, warnings should be clearly set off from the rest of the text by indentation, boldface, all caps, or other means so that they stand out.

LAYOUT AND DESIGN Visually friendly instructions are easier to follow and result in fewer errors. You can use layout, bullets, and text enhancements, such as boldface, different type sizes and fonts, underlining, and so forth, to make your instructions more readable. Layout clarifies relationships. For example, a set of computer instructions might list user actions in the left column and the results of those actions in the right column:

Press F10 and ENTER	The main menu appears.
Move the cursor to "Edit" and press ENTER.	The edit menu appears.
Move the cursor to "Block" and press ENTER	The block menu appears.

These instructions take volunteers step-by-step through the telemarketing process of a fundraising phone call. The instructions assume the presence of staff members who can supply needed materials, answer unusual questions, and so forth.

INSTRUCTIONS FOR VOLUNTEERS: 1996 LOYALTY COLLEGE PHONE-A-THON

Starts by acknowledging value of volunteers' work before requesting adherence to procedures

Thank you for contributing your time to the 1995 phone-a-thon. We hope that these instructions will help you feel at ease in talking to your fellow Loyalty alumni and will ensure that all contributions made by phone tonight will be properly recorded. Your careful attention to these details will help make the phone-a-thon a success.

Before You Call

- Read these instructions through to the end. If you have any questions, ask one of the Loyalty staff.

Takes the place of a parts list

- Make sure you have at least 20 blue alumni data cards, with the response box in the upper right corner blank, and 20 blank credit charge forms.

  NOTE: *If you have data cards on which either of the spaces in the response box has been filled in, do not phone these alums—they have already been contacted. Return these cards to a Loyalty staff member and get new ones.*

When You Reach the Alum

Offers script to help volunteers avoid fumbling when trying to recall key points of pitch

"Hello, Mr./Ms. [last name]. This is [state your name] of the class of [state your year] from Loyalty College.

"Tonight Loyalty is having its annual fundraising phone-a-thon and hundreds of us are phoning other Loyalty alumni to ask for contributions.

"As you may know, Loyalty now has over 5,000 students. We're planning to add a new student center this year to replace Healy Hall, which was built to serve only about 2,000 students. Can we count on you to make campus life better for future Loyalty students?"

If the Alum Says No

Combines step-by-step instructions with more of the volunteer's "script"

- DON'T try to convince him or her to contribute.
- "Thank you for considering our request. We hope that you will be able to contribute to future fundraising drives. May we verify your current mailing address?"
- Cross out any incorrect information and write the changes in the update section of the blue data card.
- "Thank you."

- PUT AN "X" IN THE "NO" SQUARE OF THE RE-
  SPONSE BOX IN THE UPPER RIGHT-HAND COR-
  NER OF THE BLUE DATA CARD.

If the Alum Says Yes

- PUT AN "X" IN THE "YES" SQUARE OF THE RE-
  SPONSE BOX IN THE UPPER RIGHT-HAND COR-
  NER OF THE BLUE DATA CARD.
- Find out how much he or she wants to contribute:
  "Thank you very much. We hope to reach 3,000 Loyalty
  graduates tonight. If you could contribute at least $100,
  we may be able to raise $300,000 tonight toward the
  estimated $11 million the new student center will cost.
  What would you like to contribute to the Loyalty Fund?"
- RECORD THE AMOUNT OF THE CONTRIBUTION ON
  THE LINE BELOW THE "YES" SQUARE ON THE
  BLUE DATA CARD.
- Verify the contributor's current address. Write any ad-
  dress corrections in the update section of the data card.
- Ask if the alum wishes to pay by credit card now. If so,
  complete all parts of the credit charge form and write
  phone in the signature space.
- If the contributor wishes to pay later, say that he or she
  will receive a letter and a reply envelope in the mail
  within the next two weeks.
- "Thanks so much for contributing to the Loyalty College
  Fund."

Frequently Asked Questions and How to Answer Them

**Q. May the alum mail the check right away, saving us
the trouble of mailing a letter to him or her?**
A. OF COURSE—tell him or her to make the check payable to "Loyalty College Fund" and mail it to:

> Loyalty College Phone-a-thon
> P.O. Box 28
> Loyalty, OH 41111

**Q. May the alum pledge a total amount now but pay in
installments?**
A. YES—the letter we send will offer this option.

**Q. Can the alum make a commemorative donation to
the new student center or to some other campus fund
or structure?**
A. ABSOLUTELY! Pass this call on to a Loyalty staff
member for further details.

If other questions arise, check with one of the Loyalty
staff.

Text enhancements reveal the organizational scheme. In this book, for example, chapter headings are set one way, section headings another, and sample headings still another. In software manuals, the keys on the computer keyboard are often indicated by being set in all caps ("press ENTER") or in brackets ("press [Enter]), while text appearing on the screen might be enclosed in quotation marks. Bullets or numbered lists let readers scan intructions quickly to see what steps are involved. And they let those who have already read the instructions in detail find key information without much rereading. Bullets range from the asterisks and dashes available in even the most basic word-processing program to the triangles, dots, squares, and other designs offered by sophisticated desktop publishing systems.

Illustrations save words. If your text is getting long and complicated, a diagram or other illustration may do the job better. For example, it would be very difficult to use only words to describe alternative folding patterns for a brochure or to indicate the location of switches on a control panel.

Simple, uncluttered pages are easiest to follow. Visual elements should enhance your text, not distract from it. The fancier your word-processing program is, the more you may be tempted to overuse its features. Resist the temptation! Rely on a few features, and use them sparingly and consistently.

7b A Few Points about Manuals

Manuals are collections of instructions organized for a variety of uses. Common types of manuals include:

- training manuals, which take readers through a process. They are designed to be read from beginning to end so that novices can learn how to operate certain equipment, handle customers' complaints, keep track of important information, and so forth.

- reference or user manuals, which offer well-indexed material in a format that allows for quick location of essential facts. Some examples are operation, service, and maintenance manuals. Such manuals will not be read from beginning to end; instead, they are designed to allow readers already familiar with a process or piece of equipment to look up forgotten details, troubleshoot problems, and learn unfamiliar applications.

- policy or procedural manuals, which often have a legal or quasi-legal status and which inform members of the guidelines, procedures, regulations, and outlook of their organization.

It is important to understand which type of manual you are being called on to write. Experienced programmers or service technicians will be frustrated if they have to wade through pages of a training manual to find out how to modify a program or repair a faulty part; what they need is a user manual. And burying important practical information, such as emergency evacuation procedures or how to operate the security system, in a policy manual could be dangerous.

If the manual will be a formal document that is likely to be used (with some updates) over a long period, you will probably need to consult specialists about the graphics, artwork, binding, and coverage. You will also need to refer to one of the more extensive treatments of manual writing included in the "Resources" chapter (see pp. 205–6). However, because the principles behind writing a manual are virtually the same as those for writing instructions, we offer a brief overview of manual writing here. After a look at some common features of manuals, Sample 45 offers a sample table of contents and a section of a manual that combines aspects of a user and a procedural manual. This sample covers computerized client databases, but the same principles apply to manuals for a wide variety of databases, for example, a database for processing the information gathered during the alumni phone-a-thon (see Sample 44, pp. 130–31) or a database for maintaining a list of guests and reservations for a hotel or conference facility.

An effective manual includes:

- a detailed table of contents, organized around tasks users need to perform and stated in terms they can understand. A video editor using a keyboard to add captions wants to see sections with titles like "Color of Caption" or "Sizes of Text" rather than "Chromolux II Module" or "Varifont Systems."
- an organizational scheme that breaks the larger job down into a number of separate, clearly defined tasks. Such a scheme may require you to repeat crucial information in different sections so that each will be self-contained and users won't be forced to pause in the midst of a complex task to

SAMPLE 45: SELECTIONS FROM A USER MANUAL

Below are a table of contents and a sample section of a forty-page user manual for a client database management system. The manual is aimed at novices, but it could be used by experienced staff looking for the details on a process they don't use very often. The more experienced user would consult the table of contents for the section needed and then skim the text for the relevant information.

Title makes function of manual clear

CLIENT DATABASE USER MANUAL

CONTENTS

Offers enough detail in table of contents so this short manual will not need an index

Numbers by section and subsection rather than pages to make topics easier to find

3 LOCATING CLIENT FILES

3.6 By Seller ID Code

This feature allows you to locate and either update or print a list of a seller's clients. Before you begin, be sure to get the ID code of the seller whose client files you want to locate. You can find this code in the Seller Directory in the main office.

Clearly explains function of this feature

The Client Menu below appears on your screen:

F1	F2	F3	F4	F5	F6
Clnumber	Clname	Clphone	Clzip	Product	Seller

1. Select F6 (Seller). The Seller Menu will appear:

F1	F2	F3	F4
Find	Add	Delete	Update

Offers visual displays to clarify instructions

2. Select F1 (Find). The following prompt will appear.

Seller ID code:

3. Enter in the seller ID code.
   The screen will display the following menu:

Update
Print

4. To update these files, select "Update." The Update menu will appear. Go to Section 6 of this manual.
5. To print these files, select "Print."

135

consult a preceding section. The following features will aid users in understanding the organization of the manual:

- introductions to or overviews of each section.
- a clear page numbering system. In manuals of any length, a numbering system that indicates the section number and the page within a section (8.1, 8.2, etc., or A.1, A.2, etc.) is preferable to simple sequential page numbering (1, 2, 3, etc.).
- heavy divider sheets with section headings on tabs. Such tabs are especially needed in longer manuals to help readers locate information quickly without having to consult the table of contents.
- examples and illustrations. Short examples can be worked into the text of the manual itself. Longer examples can appear in appendices either at the end of each section or at the end of the manual as a whole. Label appendices so they can be referred to easily: "For an example of a rejection letter, see Appendix II.c."
- a glossary of specialized or technical terms.
- an index, unless the manual is quite short and the table of contents alone is a sufficient guide. The index, like the headings in the table of contents, should list terms readers would use. The user of a dot matrix printer who wants to know how to print stencils should be able to find the information by looking under "stencils" or "multiple copies"; it shouldn't be hidden in the section on "Head Gap Lever."

8

Agendas and Minutes

Are you a member of a corporation's junior staff? Do you serve on an elected or appointed body in a city or town? Do you belong to a union, a church committee, a college association, or a volunteer group? If so, you may be called on to set up an agenda or to take minutes for a meeting. What is your role in this process? How much say will you have in setting up formats or changing existing ones? That depends on the style of your organization. In this chapter we supply examples of a formal agenda and minutes (Samples 46 and 49, pp. 138, 144) in order to familiarize you with the most common conventions and to make you aware of the types of questions you should ask.

8a Agendas

An agenda is a brief list of items for discussion or action by a group or organization. Depending on the group's nature and size, its agenda may be an informal list of considerations and questions to help focus discussion or a highly formal order of business. The agenda of a legislative or governance body or of any committee established by such a body may be a public legal document and may thus involve special considerations you should ask about. The agenda for a meeting may be put together by the chair or secretary of the body, by a steering or executive committee, or by a staff member under the direction of such an officer or committee.

This section begins with a classic formal agenda following strict parliamentary procedure, then offers two examples of less formal agendas.

**MONTHLY MEETING OF THE HOMETOWN
SENIOR CITIZENS COMMISSION**

Monday, January 15, 1996, 7:30 p.m.
Brennan Conference Room, Memorial Library

AGENDA

1. Call to order

2. Approval of the agenda

3. Approval of minutes of the December 16, 1995, meeting

4. Report from the chair

5. Housing Committee report

6. Medical Services Committee report

7. Report of the Ad Hoc Planning Committee for the Senior Services Fair

8. Motion: from the Transportation Committee:
    "That the Hometown Senior Citizens Commission go on record as opposing the proposed curtailment of the Elderbus."

9. Discussion of Hometown's participation in the new state fuel assistance program for seniors
    Guests: Robert Frank, State Energy Office
              Amanda Le Brun, Chair, Legislative Finance Committee

10. Old business

11. New business

12. Adjournment

Formal Agenda Format

The format of the Senior Citizens Commission agenda follows the conventional order of business as specified in *Robert's Rules of Order*.

HEADING The centered heading of this formal agenda includes the name of the organization; the day, date, and time of the meeting; the location (with no street address, since members know where the Memorial Library is); and the word *Agenda*.

BODY The order of business here is as follows:

- the call to order (the official beginning of the meeting as declared by the chair)
- the approval of the agenda
- the approval of the minutes of the previous meeting
- reports of two standing committees and one ad hoc committee
- the only listed motion (though some of the preceding committee reports may result in motions from the committee or from the floor)
- a discussion/information session with a guest speaker
- old business, which is business postponed or reintroduced from previous meetings (listed here as an open category, but agenda could list specific items of old business expected to be taken up)
- new business, which is business introduced from the floor
- adjournment (here without a specified time)

Writing an Agenda

On the one hand, the agenda and minutes of governmental bodies (both elected and appointed), of unions, and of some corporate boards and committees may have the status of legal documents and thus will have well-established formats that you must follow precisely. Such organizations often have rules and procedures that are defined in a constitution, by-laws, or some outside authority on parliamentary procedure such as *Robert's Rules of Order*. Using such authorities requires plenty of preparation. Consult your organization's by-laws or the person designated as parliamentarian. You definitely should not write legally binding agendas or minutes without official guidance.

Less formal agendas and minutes, on the other hand, will allow you much more leeway. For example, you may find that the established formats are difficult to work with, or you may be working with a volunteer group or small organization that has no set format. In either case, you may want to devise a uniform or more accessible format. Even in a less formal setting, though, this is not a decision you can make on your own. Agendas and minutes, however informal, stand as official records of a group, and the group itself or its presiding official must approve any formats you propose. This chapter offers less formal examples of agendas and minutes (Samples 47 and 48, pp. 141, 143) that can serve as models for such formats.

PARTS OF AN AGENDA   An agenda is a kind of blueprint for a meeting, a list of the items to be considered, in the order in which they will be taken up.

Make sure the heading of the agenda includes the full official name of the organization; the day, date, and time of the meeting; the location (including street address if the meeting is open to the public or if members are unfamiliar with the location); and the word *Agenda*.

The agendas of most formal organizations follow more or less closely the following standard order of business as prescribed by *Robert's Rules of Order*:

- call to order—sometimes omitted, so check the custom of your group
- approval of the agenda, including any changes in the order in which items will be reported or discussed.
- approval of minutes of the previous meeting (or reading and approval if the group's custom is to read the minutes aloud at the meeting before voting approval)
- reports of officers, boards, and standard committees (often in an order specified in the group's operating rules)
- reports of special or ad hoc committees
- motions from standing committees (often in a specified order)
- motions from ad hoc committees
- other topics specified on the agenda
- old business—unfinished or postponed business from previous meetings (may be listed on agenda or may arise from the floor)
- new business introduced from the floor
- adjournment (may list a specific time, depending on the custom of the group)

In a small organization like the Avon Theatre Company (ATC) where members know each other well, the agenda may appear in memo form. Since Steering Committee membership rotates, the memo lists by first name all current members.

From:	Liz
To:	Debbie, Charlie, Kirk, Rosaria, Abdul, Paul, and Velma
Subject:	ATC Steering Committee Meeting
Date and Place:	Tuesday, April 12, 10:00–11:30 A.M., Staff Lounge

Gives first names only—agenda is informal

Doesn't spell out name

AGENDA

1. Minutes of the March meeting. 5 min.
   Please check the financial statistics especially for accuracy, since the minutes need to go in the April 20 newsletter.

   Sets time limits for each item to enhance efficiency

2. Reports. 20 min.
   Paul: update on the Evans Corporation grant
   Debbie: meeting with the mayor's Arts Council
   Volma: recruitment of summer interns
   Any other reports or announcements?

   Follows general order of more formal meetings

3. Discuss possible coproductions with Proscenium. 45 min.
   a. Can we identify any other benefits besides what we talked about last time? Other problems?
   b. Do we like Proscenium's idea that we would handle publicity and ticket sales in return for a 60 percent share of profits? Is this enough compensation for our staff time? What problems can we foresee?
   c. Should we hire a lawyer to draw up a formal contract? Other considerations?

   Uses short name of Proscenium Productions

   Lists questions to get committee members thinking ahead about the issues

4. Assignment of duties for the next three productions. 10 min.
   Here are some suggestions as a starting point:
   Business sponsorships—Charlie
   Intern supervision—Velma
   Ticket sales—Rosaria
   Publicity—Kirk

   Lists no formal motions; group is expected to arrive at a consensus

5. New issues? 10 min.

   Allows time for additional news, issues, etc.

In less formal organizations, the executive or agenda committee, the chair, or the secretary may have an active role in ordering the agenda. For example, you may find it more efficient to schedule essential but routine or noncontroversial items early in the meeting to make sure that lengthy discussions of controversial issues do not prevent action on these items. Where it is not in conflict with an organization's rules or customs, you may wish to list time limits for the discussion of each agenda item (see Sample 47). But note that determining what those limits are is the task of the presiding officer or executive committee, not the agenda writer.

FORMAT AND LAYOUT To make the agenda easy to read, most groups adopt a standard format for their agendas. Usually, you should number all items, including the call to order and the adjournment. If the group's customs allow, you can use white space, indentation, and boldface type to make the agenda an easy-to-follow visual map of the meeting.

ATTACHMENTS Since an agenda is a brief list of what the meeting will cover, keep it to a page or two by assigning detailed information to attachments. A brief motion may appear in full in the agenda (as in Sample 46, Item 8), but a lengthy one should be relegated to an attachment. Label each attachment by the number of the agenda item to which it refers: e.g., "Attachment to Item 8," and arrange attachments in the same order as agenda items.

AUDIENCE AND STYLE Since the formal agenda of a large organization or official committee may have actual legal status and may be available to the public as well as the membership, the style should be formal, neutral, and unambiguous. Refer to members of the organization by their titles as well as their names ("Secretary Charles Larkin," "Finance Committee Chair Carol Hurston,") or by titles alone, if that is the practice of the organization ("the Secretary," "the Chair of the Finance Committee"). Give full names of committees and organizations referred to ("the Physical Plant Committee," not "the PPC").

For the agenda of a smaller, less formal organization, particularly a volunteer group, try a more familiar and personal style to encourage members to think of the meeting as a constructive, friendly gathering they'll want to attend. You may want to use questions, first-name references, and acronyms or short forms of names.

In a small volunteer group like this, an agenda is not a public document but simply an attempt to focus discussion. The tone is informal and personal, and questions rather than formal motions guide the discussion.

PLAYGROUND COMMITTEE MEETING

Monday, February 12, 7:00 p.m.

Marcy Roberts' house, 512 Vista Avenue (red house with black shutters, corner of Lucy Lane)

Includes full directions, since group meets at different houses each time

NOTE: *Please be on time. Most of us have to leave by 9:00. Please call Peggy (235-6009) or Marcy (545-3434) if you can't make it.*

Makes friendly request for promptness

1. Gary: information from Creative Play Structures and Climbs and Slides. Gary hopes to have brochures and costs available at the meeting.

2. Marcy: what the Safety Task Force and the city lawyer said. It looks like the Metal Monster will have to come down.

   Schedules reports before discussions and decisions, as in formal minutes

3. Frank and Charlene: what they thought of the Paramount structure at the Jefferson school and the Kiddiekraft set-up at the Carrolltown playground. Has anyone else had a chance to go see either of these?

4. What next? Do we want to investigate more equipment, or are we ready to choose among the six pieces we've already looked into? If we want to investigate more, who's willing to do the work?

   Uses informal and personal tone

5. When do we think we'll be ready to make a proposal to the whole PTA? Rebecca is getting anxious.

8b Minutes

Formal minutes record what happened at a meeting in chronological order, sometimes recording only the major actions taken by a group (as in Sample 49, p. 144) and sometimes add-

HOMETOWN SENIOR CITIZENS COMMISSION

Minutes of the Monday, January 15, 1996, Meeting

Present: Commission members Adams, Carlucci, DuBoise, Goldstein, Hopkins, Jaworski, O'Brien, Robson, and Yee. Guest: Robert Frank, State Energy Office.

1. The regular monthly meeting of the Hometown Senior Citizens Commission was held on January 15, 1996, in Memorial Library. Chair Robson called the meeting to order at 7:35 P.M.
2. The agenda was approved as presented.
3. Minutes of the December 16, 1995, meeting were approved as corrected.
4. Chair Robson announced that Senior Center Manager Joyce Albert would report to the Commission in February on steps taken to address complaints about the Center.
5. Mr. Jaworski, Chair of the Housing Committee, reported that the Committee will mail its housing survey to Hometown seniors next week and expects to present the results at the Commission's April meeting.
6. Ms. Adams, Chair of the Medical Services Committee, had no report.
7. Mr. Goldstein, Chair of the Ad Hoc Planning Committee for the Senior Services Fair, moved on behalf of the Committee:
   > That the Senior Services Fair be held at the high-school gym on Saturday, May 8.
   > Action: The motion was adopted unanimously.
8. Ms. Hopkins, of the Transportation Committee, moved:
   > That the Hometown Senior Citizens Commission go on record as opposing the curtailment of the Elderbus.
   > Action: The motion was adopted after debate.
9. Mr. Robert Frank of the State Energy Office reviewed the new state fuel assistance program for seniors. The program requires 30 percent city funding. Mr. Jaworski moved:
   > That the Hometown Senior Citizens Commission convey to the City Council its support for Hometown's participation in the fuel assistance program.
   > Action: After lengthy debate, Ms. Adams moved: To postpone further discussion on the motion until the February meeting.
   > Action: The motion to postpone was adopted.
10. There was no old business.
11. There was no new business.
12. The meeting adjourned at 10:15 P.M.

Winston Yee, Secretary
January 21, 1996

ing a detailed account of the debates on these actions. Less formal minutes may be chronological, or they may summarize discussions or decisions in logical order, grouping similar points made at different times during the meeting (as in Sample 50, p. 148).

As with agendas, it's crucial to learn the rules and precedents of your group and to seek appropriate approval for any changes in format or layout that you wish to initiate.

Format for Formal Minutes

Like formal agendas, formal minutes are also highly conventional in format. The minutes have to follow the meeting's agenda, devoting an item in the minutes to each item in the agenda. (See Sample 46, p. 138, for this meeting's agenda.)

HEADING The heading for the minutes from the Senior Citizens Commission includes the name of the group; the phrase "Minutes of the [month, day, year] meeting," and a list of the members and guests present.

BODY The body follows the agenda in Sample 46, since these are the minutes from that meeting. Items here are numbered to correspond to agenda items. The first item tells us that this was the Senior Citizens Commission's regular monthly meeting, repeats the date and time of the meeting, and specifies the place the meeting was held, the name of the presiding officer, and the time the meeting was called to order.

The remaining items follow the order of the agenda. Reports are summarized briefly, and motions— those deriving from reports and those already on the agenda—are recorded, showing the exact wording of each and giving the name of each mover. (In some groups, it is customary also to summarize debates on motions and to record vote counts.) Old and new business are listed, though neither was raised at this meeting; and adjournment, including the time the meeting ended, is noted.

At the bottom, the secretary includes his name and the date when he prepared the minutes.

Writing Minutes

Minutes are the written record of the actions taken by a group or organization. In small groups, minutes may be merely an informal summary of what was discussed or decided. In larger organizations, especially corporate or governmental bodies, minutes may have the status of legal documents and thus have to follow a strict protocol. Whatever the size or nature of the group, minutes may be published and therefore may also serve as a means of communicating to the wider public what the organization is doing.

ORGANIZATION AND CONTENT   The formal minutes of an official organization or body follow the order of the agenda exactly. The content is usually strictly defined by the body's own constitution or by-laws, or by the guidelines in a parliamentary handbook such as *Robert's Rules of Order*. If you are preparing such minutes, you'll need to study both previous minutes and relevant guidelines carefully. Get the advice of the previous minute taker and the parliamentarian. Still, most formal minutes are set up in the following way.

HEADING   The heading should include:

- the full, official name of the group or organization
- "Minutes of the [month, day, year] meeting"
- a list of members and guests present. (Your group may wish to list the members absent as well. It is not necessary to list all members of the public attending a large open meeting, though the names of those who speak at a public hearing may be included in the text of the minutes.)

TEXT   The text of the minutes should follow the order of the meeting's agenda. Minutes are easiest to read when the paragraphs are numbered to correspond to agenda items, but check to see if this is the custom in your group. In any case, you won't go wrong following these guidelines:

- The first paragraph should state the nature of the meeting (regular, special, adjourned, etc.), the organization name, the date, place, and the presiding officer of the meeting, and the time it was called to order.
- The middle should contain a separate paragraph for each agenda item and should show the following for all motions:
  - The exact wording of the motion or amendment.
  - The name of the mover (but not the seconder) of the motion.
  - The action taken on the motion: "adopted" (or "passed" or "accepted"), "defeated" (or "failed" or "denied"), "postponed," "tabled," etc.

NOTE: *In some groups it is customary to include the tabulation of the vote, either by numbers alone—"adopted by a vote of 12 yeas, 4 nays, and 1 abstention"—or by the names of each voting member—"yeas: (list names), nays: (list names), abstentions: (list names)."*

- The last paragraph should state the time of adjournment.
- The close should give the name of the secretary and the date when the minutes were prepared.

LAYOUT Unless the established format dictates otherwise, you can use these principles to make minutes more readable:

- Number each paragraph to correspond to the agenda item number.
- Use some sort of text enhancement (underlining, boldface, indentation) to set off the actual wording of motions.

LESS FORMAL MINUTES Less formal minutes offer you much more freedom. When a meeting is not bound by the conventions of parliamentary procedure, discussions may ramble and circle back to earlier topics. So your minutes may be more useful if you depart from chronological order and combine related points brought up at different times in the meeting. In informal minutes the emphasis should be on who said what and what action was taken, rather than on the order in which things were said.

How detailed should informal minutes be? Some list only decisions, actions, and important announcements. But many organizations, especially those that publish their minutes in some form, prefer to include more detail about the issues raised in discussions and debates. In adding such detail to formal minutes, you must name each speaker, indicate whether he or she is speaking for or against the motion or amendment, and briefly summarize his or her remarks. In less formal minutes, you may either use some informal variation of this speaker-by-speaker approach (as Sample 50 does) or just summarize the gist of the arguments on various sides of an issue without naming specific speakers.

AUDIENCE AND STYLE The style of official minutes is formal, neutral, and conventional. In an official governance body that follows strict parliamentary procedure, minutes may follow a protocol that offers little accommodation to the needs of

These will appear in the Avon Theatre Company's staff newsletter to inform the full staff about the Steering Committee's decisions.

MINUTES OF THE STEERING COMMITTEE MEETING

April 20, 1996

Uses boldface headings to organize information

Summarizes reports to serve as informational updates for readers of staff newsletter

Stage redesign: Paul reported that grant money from the Evans Corporation will be available July 1 to redesign the stage in time for *Othello* in October.

Summer festival: Debbie met with the mayor's Arts Council on April 10 about their request for a half-hour of scenes from Shakespeare at the June 14 festival. They won't be able to compensate us for expenses, but we can hand out brochures for fall performances. Debbie was concerned about the location they proposed (City Hall steps) because the acoustics will be bad. Marla Oakes, the chair of the Council, agreed to investigate an indoor location and get back to us.

Summer interns: Because of past problems with interns from Thoreau College, Velma has decided to recruit students only from Stratford University for this summer. So far she has 12 likely prospects.

Details Kirk's complaint to get staff cooperation even before a policy is drawn up

Tools and supplies: Kirk asked for a tighter staff policy on tools and supplies. He had to delay work on the *Pirates* set because all the nails and all but one hammer were missing from the toolbox. Kirk and Charlie will draw up a proposal for our next SC meeting.

Names members and summarizes remarks in logical (not necessarily chronological) order

Does not include all remarks, since minutes aren't an official record of action

Shows no official motions or votes, since decisions are made by consensus

Coproductions with Proscenium: Rosaria thought Proscenium would get more out of the copros than we would. They're smaller and have almost no publicity budget. Paul said it all comes down to numbers: we need more performers and stage crew for some of our productions, especially *Richard III*, and Proscenium can supply them. Rosaria suggested we should do just one copro to see how it goes without promising anything more. Everyone agreed. Rosaria said that if we coproduce *Richard III*, we should get more of the profits, since we'd have to use our stage. We agreed to propose that we get 70 percent. Kirk suggested we offer to include a notice of their next production in both our mailing and the play program; no one objected. Charlie said that for just one coproduction, it's probably not necessary to hire a lawyer.

Lists production duties to inform rest of staff

Duties for next three productions: Charlie will handle business sponsorships; Velma wants to continue supervising interns; Rosaria agreed to do ticket sales; and Kirk will do publicity.

outside readers, even though the minutes may be public documents. Your primary goals in writing such minutes are accuracy, observance of conventions, and clarity. Unfortunately, the latter two often conflict, since the intricacies of parliamentary procedure can mystify not only the general public but the organization members as well. The challenge in writing such minutes is finding ways, through careful selection of details and judicious wording, to make what happened as clear as possible within the formalized conventions you must observe.

In less formal minutes, you have more latitude in style as well as in organization. For group members, such minutes are more a reminder than an official record of business. If the minutes will appear in a report or newsletter sent to the general public or to other divisions of the organization, they become in some sense public relations tools. To make the minutes more accessible to both these internal and external audiences, you may add headings, bulleted lists, and even clarifying phrases following jargon or technical references. To get a feel for what will be suitable, consult previous minutes and discuss with the group or with an appropriate authority the ways in which you think the minutes can be improved.

9

Resumes and Cover Letters

If you're searching for a job, you'll need to know how to high-light your skills and background through an effective resume and cover letter. This chapter introduces the main types of resumes and discusses which may be most suited to your needs. The chapter then shows how to compose a cover letter introducing the resume.

9a Resumes

The aim of a resume is to present your qualifications as effectively as possible. A good resume will help you get to the main step in the job search, the interview. Though the format seems rigid, there is room for you to take control and present your background and experience the way you want.

ELAINE RIVERA
22 CROOKS LANE
VERNON, WI 40404
312-266-5151

OVERVIEW

Successful assistant manager with five years' experience at large branch of suburban bank. Excellent interpersonal, motivational, and management skills. Developed new personnel procedures that increased productivity 20 percent. Responsible for 15 percent annual growth in deposits in past three years. M.B.A. to be completed in June 1997.

EDUCATION

B.A. University of Wisconsin, Parkside, 1987
    Major: Economics; minor: Psychology

University of Wisconsin, Milwaukee. M.B.A. program
21 credits completed. Degree expected June 1997

EMPLOYMENT

Standard Savings and Loan, Appleton, WI: 6/89–Present

Assistant Manager, 8/91–present, Prairie View Mall branch. Responsible for teller operations as well as advertising. Introduced and supervised publicity programs to increase deposits; resulting increases of 15 percent in 1991–93 led all branches. Increased productivity of tellers by 20 percent through new personnel procedures.

Customer Service Representative, 6/89–8/91. Redesigned intake procedures for new depositors, decreasing paperwork. Managed new accounts for both business and personal customers. Attention to detail recognized by "Employee-of-the-Month Award," April 1991.

Alhambra Management, Milwaukee, WI: 9/87–6/89

Administrative Assistant in large commercial property-management office. Responsible for renewal of leases, negotiating new leases with tenants, showing properties to prospective clients.

Work History Resume Format

The most traditional type of resume is the work history, emphasizing the writer's professional experience and designed to get a job in a similar field. Like all resumes, it is organized into distinct sections with clear headings to lead the reader through the document step-by-step. (These headings can go into the margin as in Sample 52, p. 158, can be aligned at the left, as here, or can be centered as in Sample 53, p. 159.)

HEADING As with all resumes, Sample 51 begins with the writer's name, address, and telephone number, here centered at the top of the page. Boldface type makes the heading even more attention grabbing.

OVERVIEW This section summarizes skills and experience. Rivera emphasizes her successes, describing her experience positively. She briefly mentions specific tasks (even quoting increases she's responsible for) to support her claim to skills in motivation and personnel management. And while she might be shy about blowing her own horn in real life, here she toots it unabashedly—this section is, after all, virtually an ad for the resume writer. (Other commonly used headings for this overview section are "Profile" and "Summary.")

EDUCATION Rivera lists both her B.A. and her M.B.A. in progress. Educational achievements are normally set forth in reverse chronological order, but here she puts her B.A. first because she hasn't yet completed her M.B.A.

She also lists her undergraduate major and minor. While she could have omitted them if they weren't relevant, she has included them here because they support her claims about her skills.

EMPLOYMENT Rivera describes her work experience, noting her accomplishments and supporting them with specific details. Besides pointing to what she did for her employer ("increased productivity of tellers by 20 percent"), she also notes that she won the Employee-of-the-Month Award.

She describes her jobs with Standard Savings and Loan in detail because her positions there were more responsible and more in keeping with the kind of position she is looking for. Her jobs with Standard Savings and Loan come first because they are more recent. Like academic degrees, jobs generally get listed in reverse chronological order.

Writing a Resume

PLANNING THE RESUME
Good planning helps make your real abilities stand out:

- Inventory your previous jobs, with dates.
- Select your strengths and determine the weaknesses you need to downplay.
- Conceptualize your past experience in light of what you can offer an employer in the field in which you're looking for a job.
- List your specific accomplishments and skills.

ORGANIZING THE RESUME All resumes need to be organized into distinct sections with clear headings that lead the reader through step-by-step. The traditional work history resume should include:

- *Heading* Center name, address, and telephone number at the top of the page.

- *Overview/Objective (or Profile)* In this section you should state your aims or skills or both in capsule summary form, showing how you want to be regarded. Since this is the hardest part of the resume to write, save it for last. (Think of this as a "Position Wanted" job ad you write for yourself.)

- *Education* If you're a college graduate, omit high school. With some college but no degree, list college attended; if you spent a year or more, list credits completed (e.g., "University of Nebraska, 1988–90. 64 credits, including 16 in Accounting and Management"). Omit colleges you attended only briefly (alternative: "Additional study at Reed College and University of Hawaii, 1991–93"). List job-related seminars and workshops under "Education," unless you have several items to include, in which case you can create a separate section, "Professional Training."

  List degrees in reverse chronological order, with most recent first; if you're still working on a degree, though, that can follow a degree (or degrees) you've already earned. Include your major and minor only, as in Sample 51, if they are relevant to the job you're seeking.

- *Experience* Describe the jobs you've held in terms of accomplishments, with claims backed up by specific details. Include special recognitions, awards, scholarships, and offices held.

Describe jobs of minor importance with few details. Omit short-term jobs completely, unless they are especially relevant or are your only work experience. List jobs in reverse chronological order.

- *Extras* All but first-time job seekers should list hobbies, volunteer work, and even foreign travel under appropriate headings rather than separately at the end. If you've run a church or union group and are applying for a personnel opening, put this information in the Experience section. If you speak Spanish and seek a position that involves meeting the public, stress this ability in the Overview/Objective section: "Bilingual office manager (Spanish/English) seeks. . . ."

A strong resume presents experience the way a prospective employer wants to see it, with job experiences connected to accomplishments. As you plan, think of more than your previous job titles; detail the skills and abilities the jobs involved. Were you an administrative assistant? Exactly what did you accomplish? Did you increase office productivity? By how much? If you cannot quantify it, tell what new procedures you developed or instituted. Are you a new graduate looking for an entry-level office job with no experience beyond waitressing and child care? Then turn your waitressing and child-care experience into an asset: your success at both marks you as a people person, with a record of getting along with all types. As a waitress did you ever break in new employees? That is a form of training. Were you left in charge of the whole dining room? However modest, that is evidence of being entrusted with responsibility.

SUCCESSFUL RESUME STRATEGIES

- *Length* One page is the maximum for most people, including all beginners; two pages is enough for almost everyone else.

- *Honesty* Never say something untrue in a resume; it's unethical, and if you're found out, even years later, it's cause for dismissal.

- *Inclusiveness* Do you have to tell everything about yourself? No. The law limits employers to asking only about relevant experience and qualifications. Your age, religion, marital status, race, sexual preference, and citizenship are personal matters. If you have a somewhat unconventional background, it is not dishonest to omit that from the resume. (But remember that the interview is designed to uncover a broader swath of your background; the resume is just the first step.)

- *Job history* You don't need to go into detail about every job you've ever held. Some resumes set up two categories, "Related Employment" and "Additional Work Experience" (see Sample 53, p. 159). But you're not required to list every job, particularly if some lasted only a few months.

- *Job descriptions* Use positive, action-oriented terms, with strong verbs that convey the kind of attitudes employers want:

Weak	Strong
was in charge of	*managed*
did research for	*conducted research*
	researched

Use an action verb whenever you can: *organized, developed, conducted, led, assembled, acted as, investigated, planned, distributed, prepared, trained*—all signs of specific tasks. Employers want to see what you've done, what difference you've made, not just the jobs you've held. In listing jobs, don't list just the paid ones in the chronological line up, leaving volunteer work or a part-time job off or sticking it at the end. If a volunteer or part-time job gave you good experience or allowed you to shine, include it with work experience.

Whenever possible, show results:
- Reorganized forms to decrease paperwork by 20 percent.
- Doubled newsletter circulation from 6,000 to 12,000.
- Increased sales 30 percent over last year.

- *Titles* If you can honestly claim a title, supply it, even though your company never used it officially. If you did office work at Atlas Industries from October 1989 to May 1992, give yourself an accurate descriptive term: *bookkeeper, clerk, receptionist,* etc. The job description would read:

> Bookkeeper, Atlas Industries, 1989–92. Kept books and helped manage four-person office of large interstate trucking firm. Installed new job-tracking software to increase productivity.

- *References* Saying "References available upon request" is unnecessary, since everyone assumes that reference letters will be available. However, if someone influential has agreed to speak on your behalf, mention the name, position, and a phone number in the cover letter.

- *Paper and presentation* Choose a safe, conservative color of paper (white, ivory, light gray) and have your resume professionally printed or use a word processor with a laser printer, if possible. If you type it, have a professional shop copy it onto high-quality bond paper.

Functional (Skills) Resume

The functional resume is organized according to your skills, not your job history. Who should use a functional resume? Anyone whose work history doesn't give an accurate picture of skills and accomplishments: women returning to the workplace after raising families, career changers, people seeking jobs after military service, and those with a scattered work history find the functional resume particularly suitable, since it highlights their abilities, not how well they climbed the corporate ladder. However, many employers are suspicious of functional resumes, thinking that the people using them may have something to hide. Avoid this problem by confronting it head on in the Overview/Objective section:

> New Psychology B.A. with experience in counseling and student relations seeks personnel position. Pre-college experience includes ten years as successful secretary in Fortune 500 company.

Or let the cover letter explain the change:

> Ten years of engine repair in the Air Force showed me I was best at working with people, so I enrolled in training courses in restaurant management.

The functional resume breaks the link between the jobs you held and the skills you developed.

NOTE: *The functional resume is unsuitable for some professions (e.g., college teaching, surgery, airline piloting) with their own highly developed resume formats. See "Resources," p. 205, for a list of resume guides.*

First-Time Job Seeker's Resume

For most jobs, grades and coursework matter less than experience and accomplishments. But there is a special case, the recent graduate of a two- or four-year college. When judging applicants seeking their first full-time job after college, employ-

Jason Dettmer is trying to make a transition from teaching high-school English to teaching word processing and desktop publishing. His high-school experience is less valuable than his expertise in computers, so he chooses a functional resume.

JASON DETTMER
1240 ALVERNO CRESCENT
TORRANCE, CA 01999
(213) 312-2665

Uses "Objective," an alternative to "Overview"	**OBJECTIVE**	Experienced writer and computer trainer with twelve years' teaching experience seeks position as computer skills instructor in word processing and desktop publishing.
Emphasizes publications to support claim of expertise	**ARTICLES**	"Torrance Begins Computer Instruction," *Technology Today*, April 1987. "Publishing and the Small Business," *San Jacinto Register*, October 11, 1989.
Specifies technical competencies	**DOCUMENT PREPARATION**	Five years' experience teaching and using PageMaker in DOS and Mac environments. Expert in Ventura Publisher and QuarkXpress. Expert in WordPerfect, Word, and Ami Pro. Desktop publishing workshops at Vision Center, Los Angeles, 1985–1989.
Lists employment last, since it matters less than skills	**EMPLOYMENT**	1980–1989: English teacher, Torrance Schools 1987– : Word-Processing Instructor (part-time), Cal State College, Long Beach 1989– : Freelance public relations and publicity writer, Cal-Tab Associates
Puts "Education" at end, since skills matter more	**EDUCATION**	M.A. Pepperdine University, 1984 B.A. University of California, Davis, 1977

This student has good engineering credentials but wants to stress his preparation in writing and management, which will make him more attractive to an employer. He emphasizes his courses and summer engineering job and merely mentions most of his work experience.

DWAYNE COLLINS
886 VICTORY BOULEVARD, APT. 1622
STATEN ISLAND, NY 10314
718-312-2665

June college graduate with B.S. in Mechanical Engineering seeks entry-level engineering position. Background includes writing and management courses and an internship at New York City Department of Transportation. Dean's list and election to engineering honor society, Lambda Xi.

Emphasizes school record as much as limited work experience

While in college earned 85 percent of expenses; awarded New York State Regents Scholarship and Brooklyn Polytechnic Merit Scholarship.

Mentions paying for college to demonstrate record of hard work

EDUCATION

B.S. in Mechanical Engineering, Brooklyn Polytechnic Institute, expected June 1996. GPA 3.34 overall, 3.8 in major. Three advanced courses in technical writing; two upper-level management courses.

Indicates degree has not yet been awarded. Lists GPA over 3.0

A.S., Staten Island Community College, 1993.

RELATED EMPLOYMENT

New York State Department of Transportation, 1995. As intern with a design team, planned and installed backup cable system for Williamsburg Bridge. Selected from over 30 applicants for this position.

Focuses on single job that connects to work sought

ADDITIONAL WORK EXPERIENCE

Waldbaum's Supermarket, Staten Island, 1992–1994.

New York City Parks Department, Summers, 1991–1992.

Adds work experience unrelated to desired job

AWARDS

Elected to Lambda Xi, 1994; Dean's List, 1993–1995; New York State Regents College Scholarship, 1993–1994; Brooklyn Polytechnic Merit Scholarship, 1993–1995.

Lists scholarships to separate him from the crowd

ers often base their decisions upon student accomplishments. This makes sense; if you are like most recent grads, you have minimal job experience, so you don't have much to say about the positions you've held. Of course, if you have some relevant job experience, by all means highlight it, even if it's volunteer or school-sponsored work. For instance, if you were on the year-book editorial staff, add that to your work experience.

On the other hand, if you are a grad without a strong work history, take particular care to list relevant coursework. Psychology, accounting, or journalism courses, as well as internships become important links to the world of work. Also list honors (scholarships, honor society, dean's list, high GPA in your major), and all part-time, school-related, and volunteer jobs. You can include travel, languages, sports, and hobbies under the heading "Interests." Use anything you can to demonstrate initiative, interpersonal skills, dedication, and motivation—all qualities employers seek in first-time hires.

9b Cover Letters

A good cover letter helps shape the way an employer reads your resume by showing how your background and career objectives match the job opening. Don't be afraid to repeat items already in your resume; a cover letter takes the most pertinent items and highlights them. Do you have only one or two real strengths and a series of ordinary jobs? The cover letter can draw employers' attention to those strengths.

The cover letter is not the place to badmouth your current employer or to butter up the prospective employer by elaborating on the virtues of XYZ corporation. Properly done, the cover letter shows a prospective employer how to read your resume. It can also add personal flavor; the cover letter gives you space to breathe, to be a bit more informal and forthright than in the resume. (For general points about letter format, see pp. 12–13.)

Cover Letter Format

The cover letter in Sample 54, written to accompany the resume in Sample 51 (p. 152), is a standard cover letter in block letter format (though it could just as well have followed the traditional letter format).

22 Crooks Lane
Vernon, WI 40404
September 11, 1994

Ms. Roberta Ambosello
Personnel Director
Wisconsin State Bank and Trust
2114 Madison Road
Milwaukee, Wisconsin 40506

Dear Ms. Ambosello:

I am responding to your advertisement for a manager of your Springfield branch. With successful experience as assistant manager at Standard Savings, I think I have the combination of talents you are looking for.

At present I am assistant manager at Standard's Prairie View Mall branch. As advertising coordinator, I have developed publicity programs resulting in a 15% increase in deposits, the highest in all Standard's branches. In my other responsibility, supervision of tellers, my new personnel procedures have increased productivity by 20%.

I am interested in moving out of the mall setting to a bank that is more central to a community, and I am eager for the challenges of a manager's position.

I look forward to speaking to you at your convenience about my qualifications for the opening.

Yours truly,

Elaine Rivera

FIRST PARAGRAPH The first paragraph mentions the ad to which Rivera is responding and spells out the position she's seeking, since the Wisconsin Bank and Trust may be advertising more than one position.

MIDDLE PARAGRAPHS The next two paragraphs review the highlights of her career, which support her as a qualified candidate for the job of branch manager. The following paragraph explains why she wants to leave her current job for the position advertised, without bad-mouthing her current employer or singing the praises of the Wisconsin State Bank.

FINAL PARAGRAPH In her final paragraph, Rivera states she'll be available at any time for an interview. If she could only get away from her job at certain hours, she'd need to specify those times here.

Writing the Cover Letter

A cover letter should be brief and to the point, generally no more than one page. It should follow a fairly standard order, as shown in Sample 54, and observe the conventions of letter format described on pp. 12–13.

FIRST PARAGRAPH Mention the ad or posting. To minimize confusion, state as clearly as possible the exact category or job title you are seeking.

MIDDLE PARAGRAPHS

- Highlight your two or three best accomplishments.
- Assure the employer that you meet the minimum qualifications. If the ad or notice said applicants must have a B.S. in Chemistry, mention that you have one, even though your resume says so too.
- Show in more detail how your qualifications and experience correspond to what the employer wants in this particular job.
- State why you see this job as a good opportunity for you.

FINAL PARAGRAPH State when you are available for an interview.

10
Writer's Guide

Writing on the Job assumes that you understand some of the basics of English usage: what a sentence is, when to break a paragraph, how to vary style, etc. And like any professional writing book, this one expects you to have access to a decent word processor's spellchecker, even though there are problems with the best of them. Given this degree of knowledge, what's left? That is, what are the kinds of problems even experienced writers continue to have? What kind of smart readers' questions still need definitive answers? We've drawn on our experience to lead the way. Together we've worked with countless developing professional writers, some highly accomplished, some not. In this chapter we've distilled the major points those writers needed to know.

10a Punctuation

Think of punctuation as help rather than hindrance. Punctuation marks are your tools, allowing you to take charge of your writing, to shape how your readers understand what you say. That is not how most beginning writers see punctuation. They treat periods, commas, and other punctuation marks with fear, knowing that, as in math, a wrongly placed dot smaller than a pinhead can cause a reader to explode in wrath or, even worse, a teacher to reduce a grade by a whole letter. We know you probably feel pretty confident about using periods, question marks, and exclamation points, so we have focused on the more difficult punctuation that comes in the middle of sentences. For instance, comma usage is a thicket, a real tangle that depends on a feel for language as much as anything else. And even good writers need advice on using colons, semi-colons, and dashes.

163

The Comma

About commas even experts disagree. (They'd even disagree about whether to put one after the word "commas" in the previous sentence.) And if experts disagree, what should the rest of us do? Learn some of the most straightforward rules and not worry about the exceptions or fine points. And the most common rules are pretty easy to grasp. Here are four that cover the vast majority of comma uses.

● Use commas to separate items in lists.

> They praised her courage, integrity, and good sense.

> Summer brought baseball, swimming, and golf.

Some writers and editors omit the comma before the *and*. Robert Frost wrote:

> The woods are lovely, dark and deep.

After his death an overly zealous editor changed it to:

> The woods are lovely, dark, and deep.

Either way is grammatically correct, though only the former is true to Frost's intentions.

EXCEPTION: *In some long or complex lists a comma might not be strong enough to separate the items adequately, so use semicolons:*

> The main changes to the copy came from purchasing, which wanted more color; from marketing, which wanted less hype; and from layout, which wanted bigger headlines.

● Use commas before coordinating conjunctions (*and, but, or, for, nor, so,* and *yet*) to separate independent statements that could stand on their own as complete sentences. (This is called "coordination"; the result is a compound sentence.)

> Resumes list an applicant's qualifications, but cover letters point out strengths.

> Unemployment dropped sharply, the stock market plummeted, and economists scurried for answers.

But be sure the statements really can stand on their own.
    The rule never applies to longer conjunctions like *however, finally, also, meanwhile, therefore,* or *nevertheless,* which need

to be preceded by semicolons when they connect complete statements, as in the section below.

NOTE: *With short independent statements that are parallel in form, you can omit the comma.*

The spirit was willing but the flesh was weak.

With three short independent statements in a row, you can omit the conjunction:

I came, I saw, I conquered.

- Use commas after introductory words and phrases unless these elements are immediately followed by verbs.

Comma	Finally, the committee arrived at a decision.
Comma	Watching his pennies, George ordered the cheapest computer.
Comma	In fact, competitors never learned our secret.
No comma	After dinner came coffee and dessert.

Sometimes, if a short introductory element won't cause readers any confusion, you can omit the comma.

No comma   At seven he called building security.

- Use a pair of commas to enclose elements that interrupt:

Most Americans, especially those with heart problems, need to lower their intake of saturated fats.

- Use commas to enclose some appositives. Apposition occurs when the same person or thing is referred to twice (in two different ways) in adjacent nouns or phrases, like *my sister Mary* or *Alexander Zaroff, the Russian ballet dancer.* Why is there a comma in the second phrase but not in the first? Here's the rule: When what comes first is more specific than what comes second, enclose the second reference in commas.

Mary, my sister, is getting married next week.

Alexander Zaroff, the Russian ballet dancer, performs to-night.

Passions, the steamy best-seller, tops the list again this week.

When what comes second is more specific (restrictive) than what comes first, do not use commas.

My sister Mary is getting married next week.

The Russian ballet dancer Alexander Zaroff performs to-night.

The steamy best-seller *Passions* tops the list again this week.

The Semicolon

- Use a semicolon as a substitute for the period separating two closely related statements, each of which could be a complete sentence on its own.

  The management wants more productivity and account-ability; the union wants higher salaries and job security.

  OR

  The management wants increased productivity and ac-countability. The union wants higher salaries and job se-curity.

  OR

  The management wants increased productivity and ac-countability, but the union wants higher salaries and job security.

- Use a semicolon to separate two related complete statements that are linked by a word like *however, nevertheless, therefore, furthermore, consequently, meanwhile, for example, for instance, in conclusion, as a result,* or *on the other hand.*

  NOTE: *These linking words and phrases are usually followed by a comma.*

  Every consultant we brought in said we should not put a distribution center in El Paso; however, Roberta went ahead and the business flourished.

In this sentence a period could substitute for the semicolon. Then capitalize *however.* You can use either a semicolon or a period even if the "however" is placed after the break:

  Every consultant we brought in said we should not put a distribution center in El Paso; Roberta, however, went ahead and the business flourished.

  OR

Every consultant we brought in said we should not put a distribution center in El Paso. However, Roberta went ahead and the business flourished.

- Use semicolons to avoid confusion when items in a list or a series have their own punctuation.

Hillary used to send press releases to *Newsweek*, especially its Far East edition; *Time*, all editions; *Business Week*, every edition except the European; and *Forbes*.

- Use commas, not semicolons, to link a complete sentence with an incomplete element:

The indicators turned positive last month, for example, the transportation index and especially the consumer price index.

Here the segment beginning "for example . . ." is not a complete statement—it cannot stand alone.

The Colon

- Use colons after complete statements to introduce lists or quotations. Colons replace words or phrases like "specifically" or "for example" or "what I mean is."

List	The instructions could not have been simpler: turn down the heat, shut off the lights, set the alarm, and lock the door.
Quotation	The best advice about friendship in Washington, D.C., is proverbial: "If you want a friend, get a dog."

- Use colons between complete sentences when the second explains or illustrates the first.

Her rule was simple: never gossip.

NOTE: *Opinions differ on whether to capitalize "never" here; many editors prefer a capital, but others allow the lower case.*

- Use colons after incomplete statements that introduce bulleted or numbered lists.
In writing a job ad, consider:

  - your budget
  - your target audience
  - your time and resources

NOTE: *The same sentence in paragraph form would add commas and omit the colon:*

In writing a job ad, consider your budget, your target audience, and your time and resources.

The Dash

- Use a dash to make a dramatic change in a sentence, to amplify, contradict, or restate.

Postage and handling costs have reached $3,000 per week—exactly one-third of our profits.

- Use dashes to enclose inserted elements, usually a bit more abruptly than parentheses do.

The job involved forty hours of driving a week and—as if that weren't enough—sixteen hours of waiting on call.

NOTE: *Create dashes by typing two hyphens together, with no space on either side. All good word processors have ways of creating real one-em dashes (so-called because they are the width of a printed letter "M"), but most make it so complicated that few writers bother. Perhaps that's to the good; if word processors made it easier, dashes would start appearing everywhere, since some people can't resist them.*

Parentheses

- Use parentheses to enclose extra or supplementary material.

Hargrove played with the Duluth Eskimos (All Pro, 1931) and joined the Chicago Bears in 1934.

After each step below press ENTER (or RETURN on a Techno keyboard).

- Use parentheses to enclose cross references, page and section notations, and acronyms that will appear later in a document.

All scholarship applicants must complete form 16B (see p. 36 for sample) and enclose a nonrefundable fee of $40.

The report includes full data on losses for fiscal years 1991–93 (section 3.6).

The Indiana Municipal Association (IMA) voted to support the proposed legislation.

Brackets

Before word processing, brackets used to be rare because they didn't appear on typewriter keyboards. Now everyone can use them, so they're beginning to show up in more and more documents.

- Use brackets to add your own clarifying words to a quotation.

> Davison said, "America will never be the same now that he [Lincoln] is gone from among us."
>
> OR
>
> Davison said, "America will never be the same now that [Lincoln] is gone from among us."

> NOTE: *The more academic your writing, the more likely you are to follow the first example: i.e., to include both the original "he" and the bracketed "Lincoln." In both cases, the brackets indicate that you have added the word* Lincoln.

Quotation Marks and Quotations

Everyone who has studied English has been told to use quotation marks when reproducing someone else's words. That's a simple rule and a good one, a corollary to the maxim "give credit where credit is due." If you take ideas or a model from someone else, say so, in the body of the text or in a note. And when you use someone's exact words, put quotation marks around them.

The finer points of using quotation marks cause a great deal of difficulty. We give the major requirements, enough to get almost anyone by, though not an exhaustive treatment. (For more complex treatments of the uses of quotations, see "Resources," pp. 207–10.)

DIRECT AND INDIRECT QUOTATIONS

- Use quotation marks around direct quotes, someone's exact words reproduced in your work; don't use them around indirect quotes, the report of someone's remarks not using that person's exact words.

> *Direct*　　The planning commission report on Broad Meadow concluded, "This open space is far too valuable for a shopping center; we unanimously recommend that it should remain parkland."

Indirect	The planning commission concluded that Broad Meadow is more valuable as parkland than as a shopping center.
Direct	The starter said, "Drivers, start your engines."
Indirect	The starter told the drivers to start their engines.

Direct quotations give writing immediacy; they dominate in popular magazines and most tabloid journalism, where the flavor of real voices matters greatly, especially in the competition with television. Press releases and features built around interviews use plenty of quotations. Journalism teachers tell beginning reporters to include a quote whenever possible. Sportswriters don't feel a game report is complete without a coach's reaction in a quotable sentence or two.

On the other hand, much business and professional writing uses quotations sparingly, saving them for times when only the exact words will do or when the quote is particularly lively or interesting. Reports and proposals do not concern themselves with lively quotes; they make much more use of paraphrase, summary, and indirect quotation.

As in all writing, the overall rule about quotations is, you're in charge. Even if you quote someone else's words, it's still your sentence. If it sounds awkward with the quote, you're responsible; revise your sentence, or get rid of the quote, or turn an awkward direct quote into a more elegant indirect one.

Awkward	The Board of Health said, "Our vaccine feasibility study yielded uncertain results because of investigatorial bias and lack of quantifiable data."
Revised	The Board of Health said that it is not certain whether administering the vaccine will be feasible.

ELLIPSIS AND QUOTATIONS

- Use whatever part of the quotation you want. But be careful when altering a quote to fit your own sentence. If you omit words from the middle or the end, show the omission by an ellipsis, three spaced dots [. . .]. (No ellipsis is needed when you omit words from the beginning. At the end, include the end punctuation plus the three dots.)

- In omitting words, you must play fair; be sure that your omission doesn't change the meaning.

> *Fair*   *Business Week* claimed that the merger was "remarkably peaceful." (Original: "The Fortress merger was remarkably peaceful.")

> *Unfair*   *Variety* said the book "will sell a million copies." (Original: "It's unlikely that this book will sell a million copies.")

PUNCTUATING QUOTATIONS

- Put periods and commas inside quotation marks, colons and semicolons outside. (There are no exceptions in America; British usage employs single quotation marks, with most periods and commas outside.)

> *Inside*   Jonathan Swift defined style as "proper words in proper places."

> *Outside*   Thomas Hobbes described life as "solitary, poor, nasty, brutish, and short"; he died peacefully at ninety-one.

> NOTE: *Using periods and commas with quotations bears little relationship to logic. People who apply common sense go wrong here; just follow the rule and you'll be correct.*

- Put question marks and exclamation points outside when they refer to the sentence as a whole, inside when they belong to the quote.

> *Inside*   She said, "Who needs money?"

> *Outside*   Did she say, "I need money"?

> NOTE: *When both quote and sentence are questions or exclamations, put the mark outside. Do not use two marks.*

> *Outside*   Did she ask, "Who needs money"?

- With a tag like "he said" or "she wrote" before or after the quote, use a comma.

> Gardening, Anna Martin wrote, "beats child rearing, but not by much."

Gardening "beats child rearing, but not by much," Anna Martin wrote.

NOTE: *Without a "he said" sort of tag, when the quoted words merge into your own sentence, you can leave out the comma, as in the Swift and Hobbes examples above (see p. 171). You can even use a colon after the words introducing a quote, as in the example in the colon section (p. 167).*

- When a "he said" type tag breaks up quotes, surround the tag with commas.

  "Everybody talks about the weather," wrote Mark Twain, "but nobody does anything about it."

- With a quote within a quote, use single marks but employ all the other rules.

  Lee Iacocca wrote, "The day Henry Ford told me 'You're fired' was the worst moment in my life."

- When the quoted words form a sentence, begin the quotation with a capital; otherwise, use lower case.

BLOCK QUOTATIONS Set quotations of more than five typed lines of prose or more than three lines of poetry as a block; that is, set them indented ten spaces from the left margin. Block quotations are often introduced with a colon [:]. They do not get quotation marks, since the indentation shows that they are quotes.

Block quotations are very common in scholarly writing, long investigative pieces, and magazine articles. But since block quotations are unsuitable for narrow newspaper columns, they seldom appear in daily journalism.

QUOTATION MARKS AND ITALICS FOR TITLES Use quotation marks for shorter pieces: short stories, short poems, articles, chapters. Set the titles of books, plays, and films, and names of newspapers and magazines in italics.

Quotation marks	Italics
poems	*books*
articles	*plays*
chapters	*films and TV shows*
song titles	*newspapers*
short stories	*magazines*

If you can't set italics, underline.

NOTE: *Daily journalism does not use italics; newspapers place all titles in quotation marks.*

OTHER USES OF QUOTATION MARKS

- Use quotation marks to enclose a word being defined or discussed.

  The word "juggernaut" is from Hindi.

- Use quotation marks to set off words you report but wouldn't have chosen yourself.

  Every new "legislative assistant" received a furnished apartment.

  NOTE: *Quotation marks here indicate that there was something fishy about these legislative assistants. These are "scare quotes," warning readers that word or phrase is used in a different or unusual way.*

- Do not use quotation marks to indicate slang or humorous expressions.

  Antonelli is the new kid on the block in the advertising department.

  NOT

  Antonelli is the "new kid on the block" in the advertising department.

If you're uncomfortable with the phrase "new kid on the block," reword the whole sentence:

  Antonelli is the newest member of the advertising department.

- Never use quotation marks to add emphasis to a headline or title.

10b Documentation

When using research in your writing, you need to show readers where your ideas and facts came from. They may want to check the sources for themselves; at the very least they will want to see that you are using reputable sources for your information. If you are, they will feel reassured; if you're not, they will rightly be concerned.

When to Document

While you need to document your sources, you don't have to list a source for what is common knowledge. The distance of the earth from the sun can be checked in any atlas or astronomy book; it doesn't need a source. Neither does the location of the pituitary gland or the date of the Battle of New Orleans. However, when there are questions about the accuracy of the information, or when authorities disagree, then a source becomes necessary. The population of China, for instance, is commonly thought to be around one billion, so there's no need to cite a source when giving an overview. But if your work includes a very detailed examination of China's population growth or economy or health-care system, it becomes important to know what source for population statistics you are relying on. When was the census taken? What kinds of estimates are you trusting? The sources for these kinds of information are essential. (The same may apply to a figure seemingly as simple as the population of Detroit, which was the subject of complex negotiations and even lawsuits following the 1990 U.S. census.)

Documentation Styles

Everyone remembers a few lessons on footnotes in high school or college. Unfortunately, that experience won't help much when doing professional writing nowadays. Footnotes have become very rare, and even endnotes are disappearing. If you are writing for a scholarly or legal or medical audience, you'll need a guide to tell you exactly how to cite sources. The fullest guide, the 900-page *Chicago Manual of Style*, now in its fourteenth edition, is the bible of book and magazine publishers. It is written for professional editors, not for the average writer; for instance, it spends over ten closely printed pages on hyphens, more than most readers need to know.

Academic Documentation

To bridge the gap between the *Chicago Manual* and what academic writers need, different disciplines have developed their own specialized guides. In literature, philosophy, and history the Modern Language Association's *MLA Style Manual* sets forth the rules for scholarly documentation. In the social sciences it's the *Publication Manual of the American Psychological Association* that takes precedence. In science it's *Scientific Style and Format: The CBE Manual for Authors, Editors, and Publishers*.

What should the average writer use? It depends on the purpose of the writing and where it's going to be sent. If it's for an English professor or will be sent to a scholarly journal in the humanities, then by all means follow MLA style. For social sciences, use APA style. In the world of business or for a general purpose magazine that uses complex citations, the *Chicago Manual* is the way to go.

Almost all style guides are moving toward a standardized approach to documentation, though they have by no means gotten there yet. They have all virtually abandoned footnotes and endnotes for documentation, reserving them for amplifications and clarifications, and have settled on a practice called "parenthetical citation." Each time a source is cited or quoted, parentheses, usually containing the author's name and a page number or date of publication, point readers to the appropriate entry in a list of works cited at the end of the document.

For example, the following sentence might appear in an article using MLA style:

A philosophical rationale for environmental protection first appeared in Ellul (125).

The works-cited list would then include the following bibliographical entry:

Ellul, Jacques. *The Territory of Man*. Trans. Armand Orleans. New York: Harper & Row, 1979.

If the same sentence appeared in an article following APA style, the page number would be replaced by the year the book was published and the reference in the works-cited list would look like this:

Ellul, J. (1979). *The territory of man* (A. Orleans, Trans.). New York: Harper & Row.

Thus a reader can go through an article or chapter with the source list in hand and note exactly what sources the author relied upon.

In-Text Citation

Parenthetical citation with a work-cited list is now being taught in schools and colleges, and it's the model for all scholarly writing. But all along a more popular and familiar alternative has been employed in most of the popular press, for instance in *Time* or the *New Republic* or *Reader's Digest*: in-text citation. With in-text citation, all sources are mentioned in the body of the text, not listed at the end in the kind of detail used in books or scholarly articles.

With in-text citation, writers simply work the author's name, the source title, and perhaps the date into their prose:

> French philosopher Jacques Ellul, in the conclusion of his 1963 book *The Territory of Man*, was one of the first to spell out a philosophical rationale for environmental protection.

This is in-text citation; the writer has provided the source in the body of the work, and the text includes all the essential information; readers don't have to look for an entry in a list printed at the end. In most writing for a business or general audience, in-text citation is all that is necessary.

Make the citations fit smoothly into your sentences. For models, study the professional writing in *Harper's*, *Newsweek*, *Forbes*, or another high-quality, well-edited magazine that provides examples of good, everyday prose.

Oral and Written Sources

Journalists and professional writers tend to rely more on oral sources than do academic and legal writers. Journalists and promotional writers seek lively, telling quotes, selecting shorter phrases and sentences that capture the speaker's tone and personality. Or they quote statements given to them by authorities, by people in official positions. On the other hand, scholars usually take their quotations from their reading, from sources that can be looked up in a library. Rather than relying on strong quotes, scholarly writing depends on the colorless language of cause and effect. The criticism of scholarly or professional writing is that it's dull, full of hedging and qualifying, of pinning down facts and conclusions, the very opposite of a journalist's breezy manner, flashy phrases, and colorful quotations.

As a writer you get to choose the mix of references to people and references to printed sources. With quotations, less is often more. Beginning writers tend to quote whenever possible. At the professional level, quotations are included much more selectively: good writers first judge how a particular quotation will affect readers and select accordingly.

But even quotations can be overused. In some writing, the exact words may matter less than the name and position of the speaker. In an article on bicycle travel through South America, the Brazilian Minister of Tourism is an important source, even if she does not provide any delightful quotes. You might include a direct quote or, more likely, an indirect statement of what the Minister said in order to bolster one of your points or to help you set the scene; she's the kind of authoritative source who makes your readers feel they're in good hands because you've done your homework. Similarly, a popular study of mutual funds has to draw upon some authorities in the field of investing or the stock market. Again, though, quotes are not always necessary. The authorities' words are less important than the gist of what they say; often what matters most is who they are.

So if you're writing a feature article profiling a controversial political figure, a lot of short colorful quotes can capture his or her ideological slant and verbal style. But if you're writing a report telling what district managers think, their colorful language matters far less than the fact that you've taken pains to ask every one for a reaction and noted that fact in your essay or article.

10c Writing and the Law

Plagiarism

You probably know the basic principle behind plagiarism: you cannot use another person's work without giving credit. The questions come when it's time to apply this rule. What is another person's work? How much does another's work need to have influenced yours before you must acknowledge it? What kind of acknowledgment is enough?

In matters of plagiarism, the penalties are so serious that any writer ought to err on the side of caution: when in doubt, acknowledge your source. If you've looked through books and articles for inspiration, say so. If some people have given you good ideas, thank them. If you've borrowed the structure of someone's argument, tell your readers. If you're taking your facts from one or two key sources, make sure your readers know it. And above all, when you use someone else's words, put them in quotes and cite the writer as your source. (Be sure to use quotation marks when you're taking notes to indicate exact phrasing; that way you won't appropriate someone's words by mistake.)

Acknowledging the influence of others doesn't make you seem less of a writer; on the contrary, it makes you seem more thorough, more wide ranging, and certainly more generous. And it shows your readers that you are in contact with the best thinkers in the field. Acknowledgments are easy to make. If one or two people or articles or books have been crucial to your thinking, say so at the outset, in the text or in a note.

> This study takes its format from an engineering report submitted by Arlene Abbott and Frank Mansell in November 1996.

> My thinking about the role of financial instruments was guided by two experts in the field, Wes Baldwin, Vice President of Morton Trust, and Sarah Edwards, Director of the Trust Department, Xenia Bankcorp.

Note how in both cases the writer has provided a graceful acknowledgment of help and, at the same time, taken on the added authority of experts in the field.

FAIR USE You cannot use someone else's work without permission. The laws of copyright are very explicit: writers own their work for a specified length of time. Works published in America more than 75 years ago are in the public domain; you can quote them without permission. More recent works are often under protection of complex copyright laws and may not be quoted without permission. The only exception to this rule is for what is called "fair use." It is considered fair use to quote a small portion of an author's work in a work of your own. You are permitted to quote excerpts in a review or in a piece of criticism or scholarship.

Libel

Libel is saying untrue derogatory things about a living person or institution. If someone feels that what you've written is libelous, you can be sued. Corporations, large publishing houses, magazines, and newspapers have legal staffs that look out for libelous statements. Individuals or small businesses have to rely on being careful.

So how do you guard against libel? Truth is always a powerful defense. Even better is allowing for the possibility that you might be wrong. All statements that could be libelous must be attributed to reliable sources. If your notes from an interview are your source, be sure they are accurate and then keep them in a safe place. Writers cannot rely on memory; tapes and notes from interviews are always acceptable evidence, if things ever get as far as legal action.

Most newspapers and magazines follow conventions regarding people who have been in trouble with the law. If a person has been arrested but the trial has not yet taken place, follow newspaper practice and always use a word like *alleged* or *accused* or *suspected* before the name: "alleged environmental polluter Abraham McPherson." When someone is a suspect but has not been charged or arrested, be even more careful: "Abraham McPherson, suspected of dumping pesticides in the Westover River. . . ." When you do use *suspect*, be sure some official has gone on record saying that McPherson is indeed a suspect.

The British are much stricter than Americans about this whole area of libel and pretrial publicity: when a murder suspect is brought to the station house, newspapers report that the person is "helping police with their inquiries."

Libel laws do not apply to the dead, but they do apply to corporations, fraternal organizations, and most institutions.

10d Style Guides

Since the English language is constantly changing, dictionaries have a hard time keeping up. And since English is used in so many places and settings, usages change, sometimes abruptly, while contradictory spellings or even meanings become accepted. To deal with the vagaries of the language, publishers develop their own style guides to supplement bulky manuals. *The Chicago Manual of Style*'s 900-plus pages don't all relate to the day-to-day requirements of putting out a newspaper in Washington, D.C., so the *Washington Post* has evolved its own style book; the same impulse has led to style guides from the *New York Times*, the *Boston Globe*, the Associated Press, the Xerox Corporation, Random House, and a host of other organizations that use words every day.

How do style guides apply? Here are some examples:

- *Foreign names* Suppose a reporter wanted to write about the head of Libya. How does he spell the name? Moumhir Quadaffi? Kadafy? There are over forty variants of that name, all correct, since there are many ways of transliterating Arabic. Editors do not want reporters deciding on their own, so the house style guide lays down the law: Mummahir Qadaffi for that paper, consistently, in every story.

- *Variant spellings* T-shirt, tee-shirt, T shirt, tee shirt, t shirt, t-shirt, are all perfectly correct spellings. Let the style book be the guide. Consistency is the key; no newspaper wants three or four different spellings in the same issue.

- *Geographical names* Most publishers set up an authority that must be followed. You might consult the *Merriam-Webster's Collegiate Dictionary*, Tenth Edition, where the following place names are cited:

  Devils Tower (Wyoming) and Devils Postpile (California) but Devil's Island (South America).

  Pikes Peak (Colorado) and Clingmans Dome (Tennessee) but Martha's Vineyard (Massachusetts).

  Saint Johns River (Florida) but Saint John's (Newfoundland).

- *Capitalization* Should you always capitalize the names of countries and languages? Should it be *french fries* or *French fries*? *spanish omelet* or *Spanish omelet*? (*Merriam-Webster's Collegiate Dictionary*, Tenth Edition, capitalizes *Dutch uncle* and *Dutch courage* but not *dutch treat*, *French toast* but not *french fries*.)

- *Titles* How should you refer to a bishop or an admiral or a surgeon general? Most dictionaries have a section at the back, called "Forms of Address," and the *Chicago Manual of Style* offers several pages on this topic.

- *Trademarks* Freon, Formica, Band-Aid, Coca-Cola, and Xerox are among the many trademarks that get capitalized.

- *References* Should you use the *World Almanac* or the *Information Please Almanac*? the *Hammond Atlas of the World* or the *Rand McNally Universal World Atlas*? *Merriam-Webster's Collegiate Dictionary* or *Webster's New World Dictionary* or the *American Heritage Dictionary*? A style sheet directs a writer to a single approved source.)

Style guides embodying house rules are a very sensible invention. They recognize the complexity of the English language, and they tell writers that they are not expected to know everything. Good rules provide a clear voice saying, "This is how we do that here." And they point unhesitatingly to the authorities to follow, directing the writer to the appropriate spot. (Most newspapers have their guides on-line, available at a keystroke. Reporters are expected to learn the rules quickly and follow them in every story. Crusty editors won't be happy to see creativity with regard to these rules; they have enough to do straightening out ordinary prose.)

Does your publication or organization have a set of rules? If so, how satisfactory are they? When were they last updated? And if your organization has none, you'll find a selection of authoritative references in "Resources," pp. 209–10.

10e Your Computer's Professional Tools

The modern word processor has transformed writing in many ways; in particular, it has made multiple drafts easy to accomplish—writers can simply make changes and push a few buttons. Spelling has benefited greatly from first-rate word processors. Spellcheckers catch typos automatically in practically no time at all. Nothing you write should ever be sent out without being spellchecked. Grammar is another matter; grammar checkers aren't good enough yet to provide the right kind of help. In fact, there are obvious flaws you need to know about in both spelling- and grammar-checking programs.

Spellcheckers

The most important spellchecking flaw is omission. Many words aren't in your word processor's dictionary, so they're flagged as errors when they're not. For instance, among the ordinary English words used in this chapter, Microsoft Word for Windows 6.0 did not have these in its dictionary: *spellcheck* [!], *usages, workgroups, parkland,* and *craftspeople*; it didn't have *Arlene* or *Roberta* or *Cary*; it read *depictions* and suggested *depiction's,* and it suggested changing *endnotes* to *andantes.* These are not awful omissions, but they slow you down and make you think you're wrong when you're not. (*Craftspeople* is in *Merriam-Webster's Collegiate Dictionary,* Tenth Edition; *spellcheck* is not.) You'll find problems with some compound words, like *craftspeople* or *workgroup* (not in WinWord 6.0); you'll find perfectly acceptable doublings of consonants flagged as errors (*cancelled; benefitted*). It's impossible to check on a term like *chaise longue,* since *longue* (the best spelling) is not in the dictionary but *lounge* is. (In fact, so many get this wrong that *chaise lounge* has become an entry in the dictionary by itself!) The cure for these omissions is to add them to your spellchecker's dictionary. Just type carefully; many dictionaries allow you to add but not delete a word.

Spellcheckers have two other serious limitations. First, typos can produce legitimate words that are still wrong: if you type *or* instead of *of*, the spellchecker won't catch it. Second, many people confuse perfectly correct words with each other—*principle* and *principal*, *discreet* and *discrete*, *imply* and *infer*, *flout* and *flaunt*—and no spellchecker will catch these errors. If you want to get all these words right, you should set your word processor to flag your own demons, the ones you get wrong. Some word processors make this easy; some make it impossible. In short, spellcheckers make the job of proofreading easier, but they aren't a substitute for it.

Grammar Checkers

Despite all their flaws, spellcheckers are invaluable tools that every writer needs to use. Grammar checkers, however, are best left alone except for very special uses. If you have a habitual problem with an error that your word processor's grammar checker will flag consistently, and if you can get your grammar checker to scan for that one problematic item (say, a confusion between *their* and *there*), prompting you every time you use either one, then your grammar checker might be useful. Otherwise, don't bother. They're unreliable and, in fact, more trouble than they're worth.

11
Editing

Make editing a separate, well-defined final stage in your writing process. Begin by writing a rough draft to get the sense of what you want to say; write more drafts to organize your points effectively. When you have a draft that says what you want, you're ready for sentence-level editing.

In this chapter, as throughout *Writing on the Job*, we don't claim to address every editing problem; instead, we try to focus on the strategies successful writers employ. We also provide specific help on usage problems every writer confronts.

11a Five Strategies for Effective Prose

- Frontload important information.
- Use *be* verbs sparingly.
- Make verbs active.
- Build sentences around verbs, not nouns.
- Make every word count.

Frontload Important Information

Put the most important information early in the sentence. Here are two ways to do this:

- Make key actors or main ideas the subjects of your sentences. Readers want to know right away what a sentence is about. Don't confuse them by making the subjects ambiguous or difficult to find. The sentences in the weak examples below are grammatically correct, but lack force because they delay getting to the point.

Weak   One who is an experienced advertising copywriter should have developed a variety of writing styles.

Stronger   Experienced advertising copywriters use a variety of styles.

OR

Stylistic variety is one mark of an experienced advertising copywriter.

Weak   After the awards ceremony is when the tenth anniversary celebration began.

Stronger   The tenth anniversary celebration followed the awards ceremony.

- Be suspicious of dummy openers. There will be times when you'll want to begin a sentence with a dummy opener (as here). But opening most of your sentences with real subjects will make your writing more dynamic.

Weak   There were three brokers who made bids on the stock.

Stronger   Three brokers made bids on the stock.

Use *Be* Verbs Sparingly

The forms of *be* (*am, are, is, been, being, was, were*) serve as essential links in many sentences, but they are neutral and colorless. So if they show up in almost every sentence, you need to seek alternatives. Use your computer's search utility to find each form of *be*, and see if you can substitute a livelier verb.

This passage uses five forms of *be*:

> The survey that *was* recently conducted by the Chrysler Corporation's MIS office revealed that Microsoft Excel *is* the spreadsheet that *is* preferred by intensive users. It *was* also featured in the November 1996 issue of *PC Magazine*, where it *was* awarded the Editors' Choice.

This revision keeps the sense but eliminates *be* verbs, cuts unnecessary words, and sounds more professional:

> A recent Chrysler Corporation MIS survey revealed that frequent users of spreadsheets preferred Microsoft Excel, winner of *PC Magazine*'s Editors' Choice award in November 1996.

Make Verbs Active

If you overuse forms of *be*, you're likely to favor the passive voice.

Passive   The house was guarded by the dog. (The subject [house] receives the action.)

Active   The dog guarded the house. (The subject [dog] acts.)

The use of some form of the verb *be* plus the past participle of the verb (the *-ed* form or a form with a spelling change for irregular verbs) indicate the passive voice.

Passive   The getaway car *was driven* by Wilson.

Active   Wilson *drove* the getaway car.

Passive   Mistakes *were made*.

Active   We *made* mistakes.

Passives tend to make the style more impersonal, less connected to a real person, so you'll find them in rules and regulations, in insurance policies, and in official explanations, where liveliness is not the aim:

All employees *are expected* to observe regular business hours, to be courteous with the public, and to comply with the company dress code. Violators of these rules *will be reprimanded* after the first offense and *may be dismissed* after repeated offenses.

But when a high-school catalogue entry uses the passive voice to describe a course called The Craft of Writing the style isn't encouraging or lively:

Much of the class *will be devoted* to reading each other's work and the works of famous authors. Students *will* also *be encouraged* to prepare their best work for submission to local and national writing competitions.

Here's a revised version using active verbs:

Students *will read* works by class members and famous authors, while experimenting with new styles through daily writing assignments. Students *can submit* their best work to local and national writing competitions.

Remember that the passive voice is very useful; don't misinterpret this section as a caveat to avoid it altogether. Just be aware that passive verbs tend to bog down writing. The best advice: strive for active verbs and use passives sparingly.

Build Sentences Around Verbs, Not Nouns

Another obstacle to lively writing is a fondness for noun phrases rather than shorter, more direct verbs. Unfortunately, somewhere in our schooling, many of us picked up the notion that it is more authoritative to say "formed an opinion" rather than "thought," or "came to the conclusion that" instead of "concluded that." But busy readers shouldn't have to wade through extra words to get the main idea, so working writers need to unlearn this fondness for nominalization—using nouns and noun phrases instead of verbs. Look at the examples below:

Nouns   She had an understanding of the difference between the programs.

Their motion was slow.

Verbs   She understood how the programs differed.

They moved slowly.

Nominalizations always require more words and inevitably slow sentences down. When combined with passives, they congeal into what Richard Lanham calls "Official Style." Here are some typical examples:

Nouns   Introductions of new members are permitted under the circumstances listed in the regulations.

Verbs   For introducing new members, see the regulations.
OR
See the regulations for introducing new members.

Make Every Word Count

Nothing gives prose a more professional feel than tightly written sentences. Here are two ways to help you "write tight":

- Remove or replace trite, unnecessary, or overly long phrases. For example, phrases like "all in all" and "in the final analysis" are seldom needed. And others can be replaced by single words:

Phrase	Replacement
at this point in time	*now*
in today's modern world	*today*
is in obvious need of	*needs*
when all is said and done	*finally*
stand the test of time	*last/survive/endure*

Check your own writing for phrases you rely on too much.

● Reduce clauses beginning with *that*, *which*, and *who*.

Wordy   Her brother, who lives in Chicago, commutes over three hours a day. (12 words)

Tight   Her brother in Chicago commutes over three hours a day. (10 words, a 17 percent reduction)

Wordy   The advice that the consultant presented went to the board of directors, and they accepted it. (16 words)

Tight   The board of directors accepted the consultant's advice. (8 words, a 50 percent reduction)

11b Some Commonly Confused Words and Spellings

Besides crafting effective sentences, successful writers need to use words correctly. Here is a list of words whose meanings and usages are often misunderstood or whose spellings are often confused. Careful writers know the distinctions, and careful readers appreciate your getting them right.

NOTE: *Since all the words below are legitimate in the proper context, your spellchecker won't pick up errors in their use. But if you find that you frequently misuse or misspell some of these pairs or groups, you might want to alter your software to flag all instances of these words so you can check them against this list.*

accept	to receive willingly; to admit as true or valid; to agree to: We accept your offer.
except	other than; if it were not for the fact that: We completed the report except for the last section.
advice	suggestion: Please consider our advice carefully.
advise	to suggest: We advise you to withdraw your claim.
affect	to influence; to have an effect on: How will this affect our decision?
effect	result: The effect will be immediate.
effect	to bring about: The medicine effected a cure.
a lot	many (always spelled as two words—there's no such word as *alot*): A lot of things went wrong
allot	to set aside or apportion: The company allots each worker five days of personal leave.
allusion	reference: The report contained two allusions to Hobson's research.
illusion	mistaken belief: Hobson was under the illusion that his research would not be taken seriously.
brake	to stop; a device that stops something: Hundreds of instances of brake failure prompted the recall.
break	rest; rupture; advantage: take a break; break with tradition; to give a break
breath	air inhaled and exhaled (rhymes with *Seth*): a breath of fresh air
breathe	to inhale and exhale (rhymes with *seethe*): to breathe in the fresh air
close	shut; tight; near: close the door; a close call; living close to the workplace
clothes	garments: wash the clothes

discrete	separate, distinct: Once closely linked, they are now discrete corporations.
discreet	quiet, close-mouthed: Personnel staff must be discreet about workers' personal problems.
fewer	countably smaller: fewer cars
less	smaller, but not countably so: less pollution
	EXCEPTION: *Use "less" for units of money and time: less than five minutes; less than ten dollars.*
flaunt	to show off: She flaunted her wealth by overtipping.
flout	disregard; scorn: He flouted the rules by making personal calls at company expense.
heroin	the drug. a heroin addict
heroine	female lead in a drama or story; brave woman: The media called the lifeguard a heroine.
imply	to suggest: The letter implied that he would get the job.
infer	to conclude from hints or suggestions: He inferred from the letter that he would get the job.
its	belonging to it: You can't tell a book by its cover.
it's	contraction of *it is*: It's too late to change the plan.
loose	not tight or exact (rhymes with *noose*): A loose connection caused the malfunction.
lose	opposite of *win* (rhymes with *news*): We don't want to lose the contract.
principal	main; head of school; sum of money: the principal partner in the firm; the principal of South High; principal, interest, and taxes
principle	rule of conduct: She believed in the principle that time is money.

precede	go before: Johnson preceded Nixon as president.
proceed	continue; go forward: Let's proceed with the agenda.

stationary	not moving: He exercised on a stationary bike.
stationery	paper: This stationery shows the new company logo.

their	belonging or relating to them: Their profits have declined for two years in a row.
there	in that place; part of the phrases *there is*, *there are*, etc.: Put it there. There are three reasons for this trend.
they're	contraction of *they are*: They want to go, but they're not sure they can afford the airfare.

to	toward; directed toward: Give this to the director.
too	also; excessively: Order some paper clips, too. Too much rainfall caused the flooding.

use . . . to	employ: Use your memo to explain the reason for the request.
	NOTE: *"Use to" is never correct to mean "formerly did regularly or habitually."*
used to	past tense phrase meaning "formerly did regularly or habitually": The factory used to offer free tours on Wednesdays.
	NOTE: *Even though we don't pronounce the "-d" in "used to," it's always required in writing.*

who's	contraction of *who is*: It's hard to tell who's on our side.
whose	belonging or relating to whom: We hired the candidate whose experience best fit the job.

11c Some Tricky Aspects of Usage and Style

Everyone has learned supposedly universal rules about writing. Students arrive in college convinced that they should never use *I*, start a sentence with *and*, or end one with a preposition. Such rules are fantasy. More important is the overriding rule: Make your sentences read smoothly and easily; just making them correct is not enough. And never let a concern for correctness force you to write awkward phrases and sentences that no one would ever speak.

I/Me/Myself

When should you use *I*? In news stories, avoid it; for everything else, the answer is simple: use *I* whenever you need to refer to yourself. In reports, phrases like "this writer" can sound pompous and insecure. If you alone investigated a service delivery problem and want to report what you did, use *I*: "I interviewed the supervisor of the Service Department." But if you find yourself constantly using phrases like *I think* or *in my opinion*, edit them out. It's clear that what you write is your opinion. Write "The main problem is poor processing of telephone complaints," not "I think the main problem is. . . ."

I **OR** *ME*? Like many writers, you may think that it's almost always better to use *I* than *me*. It isn't. The most common misuse is the phrase *between you and I*, which should be *between you and me*. Why? Because *me* is correct when it is the object of a preposition (like *to*, *for*, or *between*), even when it is part of a compound phrase using *and*. Use *I* for the subject of a sentence and *me* for the object of a verb or preposition, even when the subject or object is compound:

> My sister and I are twins.
>
> My parents named my sister and me after our two aunts.
>
> This caused problems for my sister and me.

MYSELF Both *I* and *me* have been challenged so much that confused writers often turn to *myself* as a "safe" alternative. The problem is that *myself* is correct only when you've already used *I* or *me* in the same sentence:

> I cut myself.
>
> He asked me to do it myself.

So sentences like "John and myself are going into town" aren't any better than "John and me are going into town." Use *myself* only if you've already used *I* or *me* in the same sentence; don't use *myself* to avoid the choice between *I* and *me*.

That/Which

Excellent sources on writing (e.g., Strunk and White, Jacques Barzun) give writers very specific rules on when to use *which* and when to use *that* and then proceed to ignore their advice at other points in the same book. Our advice is: if *that* fits, use it.

Who/Whom

Use *whom* immediately after a preposition: "for whom," "with whom," etc. For example, it should be "To whom it may concern," "the person with whom I spoke." Otherwise, use *who* unless it sounds particularly awkward; trust your ear.

11d Plurals

Most nouns that used to have unusual plurals nowadays take a simple "*s*" or "*es*": *antennas, forums, octopuses*. But a few words like *criterion* and *phenomenon* still require the original Greek or Latin plurals: *criteria, phenomena*. And several of these unusual plural forms raise complex questions.

Alumna/Alumnae/Alumnus/Alumni

An *alumna* is a female graduate or former student; the plural is *alumnae*. An *alumnus* is a male graduate or former student; the plural is *alumni*. The common form for referring to a group of both sexes is *alumni*, but there is no consensus on how to refer to a single graduate who may be either male or female.

NOTE: Alumna/alumnus *is awkward, and some may see using the masculine plural for mixed groups as sexist. To get around the problem in all but the most formal contexts, use the shortened form* alum *and the plural* alums. *Or use* graduate *and* graduates, *when appropriate.*

Datum/Data

Data was originally the plural of *datum* but is now widely accepted as a singular. Academic writers and editors may still insist on sentences like "The data are incomplete," but most working writers and editors accept "The data is incomplete." *Datum* as the singular form of *data* is now rare, except in academic writing.

Medium/Media

Medium is the proper term to use when referring to a means of mass communication, such as newspapers, television, or radio, as in the sentence, "On-line computer networks may become the primary medium of the late 1990s." *Media* is the plural of *medium*; using it as a singular is common in speech but formal or workplace writing requires its use as a plural: "Experts disagree on how the media have [not *has*] influenced the trial's outcome."

11e Subject and Verb Agreement

Of course you know that a singular subject takes a singular verb and a plural subject a plural verb, but thorny cases abound.

- Group noun as subject: use a singular verb if you are considering the group as a unit: "The city council meets every Tuesday." Conventional grammar calls for using a plural verb if you are speaking of a collection of people who are thinking or acting individually: "The committee disagree on what to do next." But such sentences sound incorrect even when they aren't, so it's safer to rephrase: "The committee members disagree on what to do next."
- A compound subject joined by *and* takes a plural verb.

    The travel agencies and the sponsor have canceled the expedition.

- With a compound subject linked by *either . . . or* or *neither . . . nor*, the verb agrees with the closer noun.

    Neither the travel agencies nor the sponsor accepts responsibility.

- With a compound subject linked by *and not*, the verb agrees with the noun in the affirmative.

    The sponsor and not the agencies pays the bill.

- When a subject includes a prepositional phrase (one beginning with *of*, *in*, *on*, or a similar word), the verb agrees with the word before the preposition.

The first of the candidates arrives in a few minutes.

The chapters on format need revision.

- With the phrase *one . . . who*, logic governs, but the logic may be tricky. The sentence "Sue is one of those agents who do best under pressure" means that many agents do best under pressure, and Sue is one of those. But "Sue is the one of our agents who does best under pressure" means that Sue is the best agent at working under pressure. The best advice is probably to revise to avoid the phrase *one . . . who*: "Rabson's Travel Agency offers many last-minute special deals" is clearer and more concise than "Rabson's is one of those travel agencies that offer many last-minute special deals."
- *Each* and *either* and pronouns ending in *"body"* or *"one"* (*somebody, everyone,* etc.) take singular verbs.

Everyone agrees.

Either alternative looks promising.

11f Parallel Structure

Using parallel structure means making such things as headings, subheadings, and items in lists similar in grammatical structure. Parallelism is important in all writing, but a lack of parallelism can be especially distracting in bulleted lists. For example, here's a list that could appear on a beauty salon brochure or flyer:

Modern Image Salon offers:

- French manicures
- You'll love our nail wraps
- Hair weaving for men and women our specialty
- Try our full line of hair replacement products
- Satisfaction guaranteed

The above list lacks parallelism because the first item is a noun phrase, the second and fourth are full sentences, and the third and fifth telescoped sentences without verbs. A second problem is that the first four items are specific services, while the last is an overall guarantee. Here's how the list might be reworked as a series of noun phrases listing services:

Modern Image Salon offers:

- French manicures
- Nail wraps
- Hair weaving for men and women
- Full line of hair replacement products

We guarantee satisfaction!

For more examples of parallel structure, look over the section headings and lists in this book. Notice, for example, that the five principles that begin this chapter are all sentences beginning with imperative verbs (see p. 183), or that our chapter headings are all noun phrases.

11g Gender Neutral Language

No writer consciously wants to use wording that is derogatory toward any racial or ethnic group or toward either sex. But the issue of avoiding sexist language raises some complex problems. Here are a few guidelines.

- Avoid polite terms that may convey subtle condescension.

  No The pharmacist is a lady.
  The judge is a member of the feminine sex.

  Yes The pharmacist is a woman.
  The judge is female.

- Don't use *man* or *men* to refer to people in general or to adult behavior.

  No The crime violated the rights of man.
  Stop complaining and act like men.

  Yes The crime violated human rights.
  Stop complaining and act like adults.

- Substitute gender-neutral terms for titles and job descriptions that include the suffixes *"man"* or *"men,"* *"woman"* or *"women"*:

No	Yes
mailman	*letter carrier*
chairwoman	*chair/chairperson*

fireman	*firefighter*
policewoman	*police officer*
spokesman	*spokesperson/representative*
weatherman	*weather forecaster/meteorologist*
Congressman	*U.S. Representative*

NOTE: *Some find acceptable the terms* freshman/men, upper-classman/men, *and* underclassman/men *and phrases like* freshman senator. *But if you want to avoid all possibility of offense, substitute* first-year student(s), upperclass student(s), underclass student(s), *and* first-year senator.

Watch out for words ending in *"ess." Princess* and *prioress* are still acceptable. *Hostess* is fine for a woman giving a party, but a woman with a television or radio talk show is a *host. Actress* is acceptable to most, though not all, female dramatic performers. (A few prefer to be called *actors*.) A woman who serves food in a restaurant is a *waitress*, a man a *waiter*, though the term *server* is increasingly used for either sex. The plural references for mixed sexes are *waitstaff* or *servers*.

Other terms ending in *"ess"* are considered out-of-date or demeaning: instead of *poetess, authoress, ambassadress, stewardess*, and *murderess*, use *poet, author, ambassador, flight attendant*, and *murderer*.

NOTE: *You can find helpful, up-to-date guidance on these matters in the most current college edition of a dictionary under entries such as* he, *"man"*, *and "ess." (See "Resources," pp. 210–11, for more details on dictionaries.)*

- Avoid using a gender-specific pronoun to refer to an unspecified person filling a certain role.

   No   A doctor should write his prescriptions clearly.
   A nurse should remember that her first duty is to her patient.

   Yes   A doctor should write his or her prescriptions clearly.

   OR

   A doctor should write prescriptions clearly.

   Nurses should remember that their first duty is to their patients.

Since several repetitions of *he or she* or *his or her* in a single passage can make for awkward reading, revise to make the nouns plural or avoid them.

> *No*   When a writer lacks confidence, he or she may overcompensate by using pompous, overly formal language.

> *Yes*   A writer who lacks confidence may overcompensate by using pompous, overly formal language.

11h The Process of Editing: Collaboration

In many organizations, collaboration is built into the writing process. For example, as a newspaper reporter leaves the office on an assignment, an editor may already have assigned part of the story to another staff member to research. When typing a draft of the story, the reporter will use a state-of-the-art computer system that other staff have programmed so the paper's style guide is only a keystroke away. Next, the draft goes to a copy editor, whose only job is to read it word by word for style, accuracy, tone, and grammar. And before it sees print, the story will be read again by a professional proofreader. Many public relations offices, advertising agencies, and other organizations have similarly elaborate support networks that make writing essentially a collaborative process.

The best help you can give yourself as a writer is to make full use of such a support network if your organization has one. If it doesn't, you'll need to approximate one for yourself. Find the experts who have the information you need; ask friends and co-workers to read and critique your writing.

Picking the right support staff is not always easy. You want people who really know their stuff, who can see the big picture, and who can help with details without treating shaky grammar or poor spelling as some kind of personal failing. You may need a number of people you can turn to, each with a special expertise. A good reader for tone will not necessarily know much about the stylistic fine points or the subject matter; an expert on the subject may not be a particularly skillful writer. Also, you'll need people to call on as a matter of course, not just for special cases. And you'll need to reciprocate, reading and commenting on their writing as well. In fact, a little practice alternating between editor and writer will show you just how to play each role most effectively.

In this give and take with co-workers and friends, remember the adage by H. G. Wells: "No one can resist the overwhelming urge to alter someone else's draft." Everyone wants to make changes; it's human nature. Your task is to channel the urge into productive paths. It's up to you to tell people what kind of help you want and when. If you need someone to take a brief glance to see if the tone is okay, then say so. If you want a thorough check for grammar, then ask for it (and give your reader additional time).

Here is how one writer requested very specific kinds of help from colleagues:

TO:	Larry
FROM:	Genevieve
RE:	Enclosed draft
DATE:	Dec. 14

Here's a very rough draft of my memo on the Haskins case. Before I continue, can you tell me whether I've covered every important point? Is there anything I've left out that will make our argument better? (Don't worry about spelling or grammar; I'll polish it later.)

And how about the tone? Do I sound firm enough about our claim? I want to sound like we won't back down on essentials, but I still want to leave room for compromise.

It's due next Friday, so I can make use of any advice you have if you can get it to me by noon on Thursday.

This informal memo picks exactly those areas the writer wants help on. Larry can forget small-scale editing and proofreading because Genevieve says that this is a rough draft. The memo is conveniently organized so that each paragraph covers one aspect of the collaboration. The final paragraph clearly states the deadline.

If Genevieve was sure about what to cover but wanted someone to check the details, then her memo might read:

> TO: Larry
> FROM: Genevieve
> RE: Enclosed draft
> DATE: Dec. 14
>
> Here's my memo on the Haskins deal. It's due next Friday, and everything has to be perfect. Would you check it over to see that I've got everything just right, especially the grammar and spelling?

Both those memos start from an important insight into collaborative writing: readers need to be told exactly what to look at. Editing can become too global a process, so unless directed at specific areas, a co-worker will fall back on a college English teacher's markings or will look for every grammar and punctuation mistake. If you want help in a specific area, tell your reader. Similarly, when collaborating on drafts, be sure you understand exactly what kinds of input each collaborator is expected to give at each point.

Collaboration takes a little getting used to. If you've spent lots of time getting the wording of something just right, it's natural to feel hurt and even angry when a reader suggests major changes. To make the experience easier and more efficient plan your part in the collaboration according to the steps in the writing process covered in our introduction. For example, gathering information is the first stage, so if you want to get a quick read from an expert on whether your understanding of the topic is accurate and complete, give him or her an outline or very rough draft, with a clear cover memo targeting your questions. Waiting until the final draft to ask this expert for help means that you run the risk of needing to redraft completely major sections you've already spent hours polishing. Consulting him or her in the early stages before you've worked on the fine points makes you much more receptive to suggestions for major change and avoids wasting your time.

It's also important to recognize that each participant in this collaboration has strengths and weaknesses and that roles should be defined to take advantage of the strengths. If you're good at stating technical information in simple terms but less skillful at the overall organization of ideas, you'll need to seek help in the drafting process but will be able to offer help to others in the editing stages. If you stipulate roles clearly in advance, your collaboration can be not only productive but enjoyable.

12
Resources

12a Guides to Specific Types of Writing

Press Releases, Brochures, Flyers, and Newsletters

Aronson, Merry, and Donald E. Spetner. *The Public Relations Writers' Handbook*. New York: Free Press, 1993.

The handbook of choice for many public relations firms, this lively guide by two PR professionals offers strong chapters on news releases, pitch letters, biographies, backgrounders, and speech and broadcast writing, with many examples of actual releases, pitches, etc., used in successful PR campaigns. A handbook for practitioners rather than a text, it is more up-to-date than Bivins (see below) and offers better insight into strategies and client relationships. It's a fine choice as a basic PR text if you work well by seeing examples and inferring general principles from them. If you need those principles more clearly spelled out, go with Bivins.

Beach, Mark. *Editing Your Newsletter*. 4th ed. Cincinnati: Writer's Digest Books, 1995.

A comprehensive guide to newsletter design, writing, and publication, with a fine section on layout, clear explanations of technical terms, and many handsome illustrations. Though there is a brief section on desktop publishing, this book focuses mainly on the commercial printing process. It's a good choice for organizations that can afford classy, professional printing and graphics. But if you are on a tighter budget, and especially if you are working with a volunteer staff, the Brigham book (below) is a better choice.

Bivins, Thomas. *Handbook for Public Relations.* 2d ed. Lincolnwood, IL: NTC Business Books, 1991.

A textbook, with assignments or exercises at the ends of most chapters covering some of the same ground as Aronson and Spetner's book—releases, backgrounders, speech and broadcast writing—and also offering a chapter on print advertising and more detail on brochures and newsletters. Bivins gives more insight into the process of PR writing than Aronson and Spetner, but his text is less lively and certainly less up-to-date.

Bly, Robert W. *The Copywriter's Handbook.* New York: Henry Holt and Company, 1985.

A useful introduction to advertising copywriting for beginners and a comprehensive reference for professionals. It covers headlines, print ads, public relations material, brochures, and commercials as well as how to succeed as a freelance or agency copywriter. It includes a glossary of advertising terms and an annotated list of professional newsletters and magazines useful to copywriters.

Brigham, Nancy, with Maria Catalfio and Dick Cluster. *How to Do Leaflets, Newsletters, and Newspapers.* Detroit: PEP Publications, 1991. (Distributed by Writer's Digest Books)

The crowded and amusingly illustrated pages of this budget-priced book are a goldmine of information on how to design, write, and publish leaflets, brochures, newsletters, and grass-roots newspapers. Even if you don't share the authors' antiestablishment political slant, you'll find this a sensible and friendly guide to writing, interviewing, and research; to typefaces and layout; and to planning and scheduling the production of your publication. Especially valuable for unions and volunteer and nonprofit organizations are the chapters on editing text without bruising egos and on methods and costs of printing and distribution.

Neman, Beth S., and Sandra Smythe. "Communicating Effectively in Print: Creating Brochures." In *Writing Effectively in Business.* New York: Harper Collins, 1992.

This chapter offers a helpful overview of the whole planning and production process as it works in an actual business environment: how to set a realistic schedule, get concept approval, and work with a designer, as well as how to create the concept and write the copy.

Paper Direct, 100 Plaza Drive, Secaucus NJ 07094-3606 (1-800-A-PAPERS).

A well-regarded mail-order source for a wide range of preformatted stock onto which you can print copy for brochures, flyers, and newsletters. It also offers software templates that allow you to design your own professional-looking booklets, brochures, and flyers. (Prices are reasonable for small orders, but you should get estimates from local print shops for larger quantities.)

Agendas and Minutes

Burleson, Clyde W. *Effective Meetings: The Complete Guide*. New York: John Wiley and Sons, 1990.

A valuable guide to planning and conducting meetings: designing and controlling an agenda, setting goals and keeping the meeting on track, choosing a conducive physical setting, following the natural rhythm of a meeting, teleconferencing, using technology and audiovisual materials. Chapters on agendas and minutes focus not only on conventions of format but on how these documents fit into overall strategies for particular meetings.

Robert, Henry M. *Robert's Rules of Order*. Edited by Sarah Corbin Robert. Glenview, IL: Scott, Foresman and Company, 1985.

This updated edition of the 1876 classic is *the* guide to parliamentary procedure in formal meetings, from employee and volunteer organizations to legislative bodies. No one planning, conducting, or writing minutes for meetings that result in official actions should be without a copy. Even though you may allow freewheeling discussions unhampered by formal protocol, you will occasionally need to know how to word and act upon a formal motion, and this is the book that will answer all your questions.

News Writing

The Associated Press Style Book and Libel Guide. 2d ed. Englewood Cliffs, NJ: Prentice Hall, 1993.

The most popular compilation of house rules available, this book is on almost every newspaper editor's desk. It provides a quick and simple guide to everything from capitalization to geographical names, distinctions among Protestant churches, abbreviations, trademarks, and thousands of other disputable issues that writers face every day. An appendix includes a glossary of key newspaper terms. At the end is an excellent brief guide to issues of libel, but it in no way replaces a good lawyer.

Cappon, Rene J. *The Associated Press Guide to News Writing.* 2d ed. New York: Arco Books, 1991.

You don't have to be a reporter to learn from this 162-page guide to the best in newspaper style. In thirteen brief, example-packed chapters, Cappon covers what works and what doesn't, the elements of good feature writing, how to liven up your prose, and what makes a successful lead.

Metzger, Ken. *Creative Interviewing: The Writer's Guide to Gathering Information by Asking Questions.* Englewood Cliffs, NJ: Prentice Hall, 1989.

The best book we've seen on how to conduct interviews, offering plenty of creative strategies and practical suggestions to help even veteran interviewers get better results. Best of all, it's a delight to read, with amusing Q-and-A dialogues illustrating what not to do and colorful anecdotes about the successes and failures of real interviewers. The chapter on the personality interview offers a list of 20 questions to make even reticent subjects open up.

The Missouri Group. *News Writing and Reporting.* 3d ed. New York: Harcourt Brace, 1994.

The standard text used in most introductory journalism courses, covering all the basics in a responsible, if somewhat flat manner. And though it contains more than most people need to know about the processes of publishing and newsgathering, it is unsurpassed for its discussions and how-to sections on the nuts and bolts of journalistic practice.

Murray, Donald. *Writing for Your Readers: Notes on the Writer's Craft from the* Boston Globe. Old Saybrook, CT: Globe Pequot Press, 1983.

Murray is both a Pulitzer Prize–winning newspaperman and a veteran writing teacher. His short book, subtitled *A Handbook of Practical Advice on How to Write with Vigor, Clarity, and Grace,* draws on his experience at two Boston newspapers. The brief, bite-sized chapters are aimed primarily at newspaper people. It's probably the third book every reporter should have, the first two being the Associated Press guides to style and to news writing.

Letters, Memos, and Reports

Poe, Roy W. *The McGraw-Hill Handbook of Business Letters.* 3d ed. New York: McGraw Hill, 1994.

This widely used book's broad range of letters includes requests, announcements, sales and customer letters, public relations correspondence, job applications, and letters of recommendation. A real strength is its consistent emphasis on personalizing style and promoting goodwill, while keeping writing lively and direct. The chapter on how to write acceptances or regrets to a formal invitation would make your granny proud, though most of us may have limited use for such advice. The resume chapter, though generally sound, does not reflect the most current thinking.

Resumes and Cover Letters

Eyler, David R. *Resumes That Mean Business.* New York: Random House, 1993.

Eyler gives the widest variety of examples of resume types, all presented in $8\frac{1}{2} \times 11$ inch format. Advice is sensible and down to earth, though the large number of resume types may bewilder some job seekers.

Washington, Tom. *Resume Power.* Bellevue, WA: Mount Vernon Press, 1993.

This large-format resume book gives the most help on the whole job-search process, enabling readers to see how resumes operate within the larger context. Some of what Washington provides is just common sense, while other advice allows readers to gain genuine insight into how the process works.

Instructions and Manuals

Davis, Michael, Gary M. Gray, and Harry Hallez. *Manuals That Work: A Guide for Writers.* East Brunswick, NJ: Nichols Publishing, 1990.

A good, basic introduction to all the steps involved in writing a manual: determining which type of manual to write, collecting and organizing material, interviewing technical experts, drafting, technical review, printing, and distribution. It is generally well laid out and includes many helpful illustrations and samples, though a few samples are in type small enough to require a magnifying glass for all but the keenest eyes.

12b Guides to Layout and Design

Alred, Gerald J., and others. "Layout and Design." In *The Professional Writer: A Guide for Advanced Technical Writing*, 160–200. New York: St. Martin's Press, 1991.

A useful brief introduction to layout and design, with well-written sections on the theory of design, typography, highlighting and finding devices, page design, and packaging and many samples and illustrations.

White, Jan V. *Graphic Design for the Electronic Age: The Manual for Traditional and Desktop Publishing.* New York: Watson-Guptill Publications, 1988.

Everything you need to know about typefaces and sizes, page design, text highlighting, and bindings is included in this text, whose layout admirably practices what the book preaches. Clearly and judiciously written, it offers sound practical advice on making your text readable and visually attractive, and it includes a comprehensive glossary of technical terms.

Whitten, Alfred. *The Makeover Book.* Carmel, CA: Ventana Press, 1990.

A "before and after" book for the newsletter editor, offering hundreds of simple and striking suggestions for transforming dull and ordinary to contemporary and lively. Nothing in the book requires fancy equipment, powerful computers, or a degree in design. It's simply a collection of intelligent ideas from a master layout artist.

Whitten, Alfred. *Newsletters by Design.* Carmel, CA: Ventana Press, 1994.

Offers the best explanation we know for what makes certain layouts effective. Whitten doesn't just come up with sensible suggestions; he gets at the principles that lie behind so many attractive formats, enabling writers and editors to learn in depth what will deliver their messages most effectively.

12c Guides to Effective Writing

Elbow, Peter. *Writing without Teachers*. New York: Oxford University Press, 1975.

A perennial favorite, this slim volume introduces Elbow's simple technique for unblocking. He focuses on the writing process itself and what can go wrong with it. Elbow recommends freewriting, collaboration, and revision. Not everyone will agree with all of Elbow's suggestions, but anyone can learn from his sensible advice and specific ideas for working with others and revising. This book has helped thousands to become fluent and confident writers.

Fowler's Modern English Usage. 2d ed. Revised and edited by Sir Ernest Gowers. New York: Oxford University Press, 1965.

The most famous usage guide ever written, *Fowler* has been the companion of countless British and American authors and editors. Now a generation old and somewhat dated, it is quirky, funny, beautifully written, and eminently sensible. Though the book is aimed primarily at the British market, the words "*Fowler* says . . .*" are heard wherever people discuss good English.

Lanham, Richard. *Revising Prose*. 3d ed. New York: Macmillan, 1992.

The quickest and simplest way to streamline your writing is with what Lanham calls his "paramedic method." It's not a full course in writing (for that, see Williams); instead, it's a first-aid kit for people whose prose sprawls or contains too much flab. Lanham attacks what he terms "Official Style," the kind of overlarded prose most people see every day in insurance policies, rules and regulations, or pronouncements issued by corporations, schools, and the government. Also available is *Revising Business Prose*, a more focused version.

Lauchman, Richard. *Plain Style: Techniques for Simple, Concise, Emphatic Business Writing*. New York: AMACOM, 1993.

One of the best books on improving business prose and any writing where the goal is to convey ideas clearly and efficiently to busy readers. Lauchman admirably practices the "transparent" style he preaches, organizing his book around a series of pithy rules (like "The reader reads the words, not the mind" and "In business, readers are ferociously impatient") and witty explanations. It includes an excellent section on editing, with practical advice on a number of disputed areas of grammar and usage. If you own only one guide to effective writing at work, this should be it.

Strunk, William, and E. B. White. *The Elements of Style.* 3d ed. New York: Macmillan, 1979.

Compiled by Strunk for his Cornell classes in 1917, revised by White in 1957, and arguably the most popular usage guide in America. It's really too idiosyncratic and skimpy to serve as a main source for knotty issues of usage, but it remains valuable for White's superb concluding essay on style. The fact that it is so well known by writers and editors makes it worth buying and reading; it has become a universal source, a compendium of common knowledge.

Williams, Joseph. *Style: Toward Clarity and Grace.* Chicago: University of Chicago Press, 1990.

The book to use if you want to give yourself an advanced course in clear writing. It presents separate lessons on correctness, clarity, concision, cohesion, emphasis, controlling sprawl, punctuation, and elegance. There are exercises in every chapter, with answers printed at the end. Unlike many other authors of self-improvement books, Williams is a linguist, so his suggestions have the force of genuine knowledge behind them. (For a quick, lighter alternative, see Lanham, above.)

12d Guides to Usage, Including Dictionaries

The two major sources of information on current usage are usage guides and dictionaries. While usage guides may offer more comprehensive treatments, most hardcover college edition and unabridged dictionaries include helpful notes, many quite extensive, on currently debated usage issues. With either source, but more commonly with dictionaries, you may need to look up usage notes under the basic forms of words, finding *whom* and the difference between *lay* and *laid* discussed under *who* and *lie*. While a usage guide may offer an entry on sexist language, you are more likely to find such discussions under *he* in a dictionary.

No matter which usage guide you choose, make sure that it focuses on American rather than British English and that it was written within the past ten years, preferably within the last five, so that it covers language changes like the substitution of *snuck* for *sneaked* and the thousands of new words and usages that enter American English each year. We list two important usage guides and the major full-sized dictionaries, usually referred to as college editions and available for $20 to $25 in hardcover. Every writer or editor should have one of these dictionaries within arm's reach.

Usage Guides

The Chicago Manual of Style: The Essential Guide for Writers, Editors, and Publishers. 14th ed. Chicago: University of Chicago Press, 1993.

This book's subtitle says it all. This 921-page volume is the bible of professional editors. It covers issues of style and documentation exhaustively, telling most writers more than they need to know about hyphens, footnotes, quotation marks, foreign phrases, and a host of other troublesome items. This is the guide every book and magazine editor uses every day.

Merriam-Webster's Dictionary of English Usage. Springfield, MA: Merriam-Webster, 1994.

Soundly grounded in current linguistic scholarship, with detailed historical treatment of each entry, this reference is fine if you have an enlightened editor and readers who won't look down their noses if you split infinitives. But if you are conscious of writing for those who see themselves as guardians of the purity of the language, you'll need to take some of this guide's advice with a grain of salt—for instance, its dismissal of objections to the use of *like* in sentences such as "He acted like he always does" as part of the "folklore of usage." You also may find you need to brush up on grammatical terminology in order to follow the fine points of some discussions.

Morris, William, and Mary Morris. *Harper's Dictionary of Contemporary Usage.* 2d ed. New York: Harper Collins, 1994.

A helpful reference for the working writer wary of offending sticklers. Aimed at a nonacademic audience, this guidebook offers a clear explanation of each usage question in lay terms, avoiding complicated grammatical terminology. On controversial topics such as the use of *hopefully* to mean "we hope" or "it is to be hoped," the editors report individual responses of a usage panel drawn from a wide range of fields. Since panel members tend to be more conservative than linguistic scholars, their responses offer the working writer a valuable sense of how certain readers may react to actual or perceived misuses. On the other hand, since this reference tends to be conservative, writers striving for a more conversational or trendy style may find the advice here too restrictive.

Collegiate Dictionaries

The American Heritage Dictionary. 3d ed. Boston: Houghton Mifflin, 1994.

Though not as widely accepted as an authority on matters of spelling, capitalization, and grammatical matters like verb tenses as *Webster's New World Dictionary*, this may be the most helpful dictionary for the working writer who seeks advice on usage. Its usage notes, based on the responses of a panel of writers in a wide range of fields, help writers make informed decisions about acceptable choices in specific contexts. And the advice in the notes is always practical: for example, *American Heritage* states the linguistic justification for using *hopefully* to mean "it is to be hoped" or "we hope," while at the same time acknowledging that perceived misuse of this word has become for many a sort of litmus test of whether a writer cares about correctness. It also advises that, while formal writing still observes traditional distinctions between *who* and *whom*, strict observance of this distinction in speech or informal writing may brand you as stuffy or a stickler.

Merriam-Webster's Collegiate Dictionary. 10th ed. Springfield, MA: Merriam-Webster, 1994.

This is the descendent of the original *Webster's Dictionary*; it is based on the most authoritative American dictionary, *Webster's Third International*. It's admirably attuned to the latest linguistic thinking, though the usage notes are often too brief and broadminded to alert the working writer to lingering prejudices in many readers. It is available on CD-ROM.

The Random House Unabridged Dictionary. 2d ed. Newly revised and updated. New York: Random House, 1994, and *The Ran-*

dom House College Dictionary. rev. ed. New York: Random House, 1995.

Both dictionaries offer virtually the same usage notes, which are clear and reflect current linguistic scholarship while acknowledging areas of controversy. The working writer should be aware that the dictionary's progressive views may not be shared by all readers and should pay close attention to its distinctions between what is common in speech and informal writing and what is acceptable in formal, edited prose. The unabridged version is available on CD-ROM.

Webster's New World Dictionary. 3d ed. New York: Macmillan, 1994.

Recognized by the Associated Press, *The New York Times*, and many professional editors as the first authority on matters such as capitalization, hyphenation, spelling, and forms of words, this dictionary is not very revealing about how certain usages may be received by readers. The status of *like* to mean "as if" is revealed only in labeling the usage colloquial, and the use of *hopefully* to mean "It is to be hoped" is simply included as legitimate without comment. A CD ROM version is available.

12e Computers and Writing

Microsoft Word for Windows.

The current state of the art word-processing program. The previous leader, WordPerfect, which made the transition to Windows less successfully, remains a fine program with millions of adherents. But Word for Windows defines the best a program can be, at least for the present. It has consistently won *PC Magazine*'s Editors' Choice Award. It also has the best after-market guide, the *Cobb Group's Word 6 for Windows Companion* (Microsoft Press, 1994).

Microsoft Publisher.

Far and away the best cheap desktop publishing program, it "fits" into Word for Windows, making it seem like an extension of the word processor, a great advantage. And its "wizards" enable you to set up newsletters or letterheads or many other formats almost effortlessly. For the entrepreneur or small-office manager, Microsoft Publisher will solve just about every simple formatting problem that comes up.

QuarkXpress and PageMaker.

The professional programs of choice. Everything else, including a fine program like Microsoft Publisher, falls well short of these industrial-strength programs. They're difficult to master, so, for best results, take a course in one or the other. But once you've learned one, there's nothing else that can provide similar versatility and flexibility. You can produce top layout with either, though QuarkXpress seems to be gaining in popularity. Both were once primarily Macintosh programs, but are now equally at home on PCs. Knowing either one will give any writer or editor an extra edge in talking to production people.

Copyedit.

An internet newsgroup dedicated to the world of copyediting, it regularly has some 200 U.S. copyeditors drop in to ask and answer questions about knotty grammatical or usage problems and also to talk to each other about the latest news in the world of copyediting. It's pretty much a free-for-all. A new member signing on can read the exchanges for a while (the term is *lurk*), then plunge in with a question, answer, or anecdote. This is the place to go if you have a complex question that cannot be solved by the *Chicago Manual*. It's expert help for free. (The address is: copyedit@cornell.edu.)

Index